## Endorsements for SPECIAL EDUCATION 2.0— Breaking Taboos to Build a NEW Education Law

This little book packs a hell of a punch. I predict that readers will be alternately amazed, slack-jawed, angry, and optimistic about the future of public education--if we are smart enough to take the advice of a real expert, Miriam Freedman, and work together to make education special for all students. *Special Education 2.0* is common sense thinking at its best.

John Merrow, former Education Correspondent, PBS NewsHour, and founding President, Learning Matters, Inc.

∎ ∎ ∎

Miriam Freedman is a seed planter of ideas. She describes eloquently what *could be* in the field of special education that is long overdue for a revision, or rather, a transformation! If you are among the many hundreds of thousands of educators and parents who believe we can do better for our students with disabilities, I highly recommend reading *Special Education 2.0* so that you see her vision and perhaps even be part of its transformation.

Steven R. Sandoval, PhD, Executive Director of Special Services, Westminster Public Schools, CO, 2016 Honoree, Education Week

*From

After celebrating special education's success in providing education access for all students with disabilities over the past 40+ years, attorney Miriam Freedman takes a long overdue look at today's reality—filled with legal and damaging dysfunction, strangling bureaucracy and litigation. Refreshingly, she creates a vital blueprint for an inclusive, positive new law for all students—general and special education. *Special Education 2.0* should start a national conversation to liberate educators, parents, and students from this broken system. I am happy that Ms. Freedman has shared her wide experience in this compelling little book— a must-read for anyone interested in improving education.

Philip K. Howard, Chair of Common Good and author of
*The Rule of Nobody*

■ ■ ■

This important book raises vital issues that we need to confront in public education—if we ever want to truly improve it for all students. Miriam Freedman has done us a great service by getting the long overdue conversation started. Let's talk!

Esther Wojcicki, Founder of Palo Alto High Media Arts Center &
former Chair of Creative Commons

■ ■ ■

Some areas of public policy become so contentious that it is difficult to bring rational consideration to them. Special education has been such an area for the four decades since federal legislation first addressed the issue. Nonetheless, over this time, Miriam Freedman has continued to provide both wisdom and common sense to policies. Now she reaches a startling conclusion: Fixing it is not possible. We need to replace how we deal with special education. Policy makers need to pay serious attention to this idea.

Eric A. Hanushek, PhD, Hoover Institution, Stanford University

■ ■ ■

Miriam Freedman once again offers us opportunity to contemplate special education reform. She invites each of us to join in conversation, to think BIG, and to dream aloud. Now is the time. With the "reauthorization" of IDEA looming, all educators, parents, and community members are called to be part of this brave conversation. These 5 directions will give structure to some bold and contemplative interaction that could lead to enlightened, positive, reformative action. Special Ed 2.0 is just beyond the horizon. Use this book to start the conversation or join a discussion. Together, we can break taboos and close in on a better education law for all students.

Anne Delfosse, Executive Director, West Orange County Consortium
for Special Education

■ ■ ■

I heartily agree with Miriam Freedman's focus on reforming a forty-year old law for our twenty-first century schools. This conversation ought to happen and I always appreciate —even if I don't always agree with— Freedman's provocative proposals for reform.

William S. Koski, JD, PhD, Professor of Law and Professor of Education (by courtesy), Stanford University Law School

■ ■ ■

In *Special Education 2.0*, Miriam Freedman has marvelously provided a blueprint for shifting the conversation about special education in the 21st Century. Her thesis that schools must focus attention, efforts, and resources in support of all students, and on creating learning environments that focus more on individual student strengths and less on labels, would provide benefits for all.

Steven Stone, Superintendent of Schools, Dracut Public Schools

■ ■ ■

No one will agree with every idea in this courageous, taboo-shattering book. But as a conversation-starter, it's exactly what we need: a call to re-imagine special education and general education from top to bottom, rather than remain boxed-in by the past. Let the debate begin!

Michael J. Petrilli, President, Thomas B. Fordham Institute

## Also by Miriam Kurtzig Freedman, JD, MA

*Fixing Special Education: 12 Steps to Transform a Broken System*
(2009, reprinted in 2010)

*Grades, Report Cards, Etc...and the Law*
(2005, 2008, 2010, reprinted in 2016)

*IEP and Section 504 Team Meetings...and the Law*
(2008, 2010)

*Meeting NCLB's Mandate: Your Quick-Reference Guide to
Assessments and Accountability* (LRP Publications 2nd ed., 2008)

*Student Testing and the Law*
(LRP Publications, 2001, 2004, 2005)

*LEGALESE—The Words Lawyers Use and What They Mean*
(Dell Publishing, 1990)

*A Sourcebook for Substitutes and Other Teachers,* with Teri Perl
(Addison Wesley, 1974, with many reprints)

# SPECIAL EDUCATION 2.0

# SPECIAL EDUCATION 2.0

## Breaking Taboos to Build a NEW Education Law

### Miriam Kurtzig Freedman, JD, MA

**What if** we build schools that *really* focus on teaching and learning for *all* students—general and special education—and go beyond merely tweaking today's broken system?

**What if** we finally have a national conversation to build a new law and dream BIG?

Why dream? Dreams have power and can inspire.[1]  Even if you, my dear readers, don't agree with everything—or anything—in *SPECIAL EDUCATION 2.0*, I hope you agree that it's time to start that conversation.

But, I'm getting ahead of the story.

# Contents

## Preface—Why I wrote this book and principles for a NEW law

Paradoxically, the roots of this book are both deep and rather recent. They begin with my father who died when I was seven years old and gathered steam after talking with my friend, Dave, at the café. Let me explain.

I was born in Palestine (now Israel). My father had been a lawyer in Germany. In the 1930s, he was forced to leave and went to Palestine. There, he became a farmer in a village near Haifa, where he met my mother. He was a serious man and often spoke up at meetings, voicing concerns about village governance and finances.

In 1948, after a long illness, he died. Within a year, my mother, brother, and I began our move to the United States (US). I became a teacher, then a lawyer. I also got married and have two children and a grandchild. In short, I'm living the good life.

Imagine my surprise when, in 2006, almost sixty years after my father died, a woman from that very village wrote a history of its first fifty years. In it, she quoted him and his ideas at those public meetings. I was so moved and, I have to admit, proud.

The reality is that he died much too young, as a "nobody." Yet, his ideas lived on. People remembered them. I learned that *ideas* matter—a lot. You picked up *Special Education 2.0—Breaking Taboos to Build a NEW Education Law* because *you* have ideas and dreams; you care deeply.

I have worked in education and law for almost fifty years—as a teacher, hearing officer, lawyer, and reformer. And, as you can imagine, I have a vision and ideas about how to move forward. Furthermore, thanks to my father, I believe that we can have an influence and make a difference far beyond what we may imagine today. Ideas impact the future in ways we can't possibly know. They *do* live on.

And, you may ask, what about the café?

There we were at the café in the heart of Silicon Valley on a sunny Sunday in 2014. Just Dave, another café regular, and me. I was grumbling about the many flaws in the federal special-education law that serves some 13–14 percent of students in US schools. I lamented that special ed, as special education is also called, often provides services to struggling students too late, that it impacts all students and is too bureaucratic, adversarial, and not outcome-based, for starters. The law I was talking about is the IDEA (Individuals with Disabilities Education Act), enacted in 1975.

Dave, who is not involved with special education at all, said, "So, stop complaining and write a new law. Write it the way you want it to be. Just do it!"

"Write a new law? Wow. Can I?"

"Yes! Make it brief and pithy. Get input from others. Then go out and do lectures and seminars on it. And go to Washington." Dave made it sound so easy.

I had just moved to Silicon Valley. Obviously, it was time to catch on to this land of "Just do it!" Disrupt and create anew. Here, each new creation gets a higher number. Thus, the new law's name is SPECIAL EDUCATION 2.0.

Putting these two stories together led me to write this book. Looking for new ideas is probably why you picked it up. It is time for us to let go of taboos, be provocative *and* caring, and work together to build a NEW education law—something I'm kicking off with this book and the proposed new law. If you believe, as I do, that we can do better for our students and nation, let's get this conversation moving.

The next few pages are the new law's proposed Preamble and Guiding Principles.

■ ■ ■

# SPECIAL EDUCATION 2.0—
## Preamble and Guiding Principles

### **Preamble**

Our nation needs public education to meet the needs of *all* students. We need to educate students through research-based methods built on excellence and equity principles, and we need a law that clearly identifies the responsibilities and roles of all parties involved—educators, parents, and students. And finally, we need an education system that does not rely on an individual entitlement in order to get educational services to students.

### **Guiding Principles**

SPECIAL EDUCATION 2.0 begins with a laser focus on improving general education outcomes for *all* students. Here are its five essential principles, herein called "Directions."

- Equity and excellence for all students; for example, not letting mainstreaming/ inclusion get in the way of education without objective, supporting evidence;
- New realities and reforms with research-based instruction for students with disabilities;

- Shared responsibilities and clear roles for educators, parents, and students;
- New governance design and structure with no individual entitlement; and
- Honor the success of the current special-education law, herein called "SPECIAL ED 1.0."

## DIRECTION 1: Equity and excellence for all students

This new law, SPECIAL EDUCATION 2.0, also shortened to SPECIAL ED 2.0, is built on this truth: *Laws don't educate; teachers do.* This law frees teachers to do just that—with support and honor, without strangling paperwork and compliance requirements. This new law prioritizes orderly instruction in classrooms and advocates partnering with parents to do their part.

SPECIAL ED 2.0 focuses on *school readiness.* It promotes a home-based, parent-engaged learning environment, along with preschool approaches to help many children close language development and other gaps before they start school.

SPECIAL ED 2.0 applies *challenging standards* and *curricula* and ensures that standards are, in fact, challenging. Adaptations (accommodations or modifications) are used to improve learning, not just to get kids "through." It avoids doublespeak and promotes the use of plain language.

SPECIAL ED 2.0 invites us to enhance equity and excellence by "Thinking Different," as Apple exhorted us to do, about schools and learning. We can learn from other countries and from evolving views about abilities and disabilities in our own country.

SPECIAL ED 2.0 builds equity in funding by placing spending caps on special education, funding only research-based programming, and collecting and disseminating cost data. Its goal is to create equitable funding to meet the needs of all students so they can grow and learn, based on their current performance.

**DIRECTION 2: New realities and reforms with research-based instruction for students with disabilities**
Currently in US schools, the reality is that there are two groups of students with disabilities. The larger group (80–90 percent of all students with disabilities) includes students with generally mild and moderate disabilities. Students in the second, much smaller group (10–20 percent, or about 1–2 percent of all students) have severe or profound needs.

For students with generally mild and moderate disabilities, this new law challenges current practices and beliefs through early interventions for struggling students. The new law follows effective practices in Finland and in some United States schools, such as those in Westminster, Colorado. It uses the "growth mindset" approach and diagnoses and labels students only after instruction, as reflected through various tiers of support and other interventions, has been determined ineffective. For the most part, this new law focuses on the group of students with generally mild and moderate disabilities.

Because the needs of students with severe or profound disabilities are generally more complex and costly than those in the larger group, this new law recommends that a task force help forge a new way for them. Of course, these students are part of *all* students as that term is used herein. It's their needs that require a new approach, to be determined after the task force concludes its work.

SPECIAL ED 2.0 focuses on the mission of schools to educate and include students in general-education programs, as appropriate for their and their peers' learning and using research-supported approaches and practices.

This new law shifts the Least Restrictive Environment (LRE) approach, which focuses on location, to a Least Intervention Needed (LIN) approach, which focuses on current student needs. It follows the mantra, "First, do no harm." In addition, it highlights student strengths, as well as weaknesses.

SPECIAL ED 2.0 focuses on classroom management (often called "discipline") to ensure a positive learning environment for all.

### DIRECTION 3: Shared responsibility and clear roles for educators, students, and parents

For educators and other service providers, this new law builds more time on-task by lessening teachers' load for other responsibilities. It strengthens teacher preparation and provides resources, emphasizing curriculum competence and research-supported approaches to improve student outcomes. It builds trust with students and parents through plain language principles. It recognizes that sometimes other public agencies (health, welfare, judicial, and so on) need to be involved, and it requires their engagement.

For students, this new law focuses on student engagement—their responsibility to learn, to be motivated, to be present.

For parents, this new law focuses on building parent engagement and informing parents of their responsibility for school readiness. It relies on clear communication and trust–building, and it values all participants at school and home.

**DIRECTION 4: New governance structure and collaboration with no individual entitlement**

SPECIAL ED 2.0 builds in local-control flexibility as now does the 2015 federal law for general education, Every Student Succeeds Act (ESSA). It focuses on positive relationships and provides trust-building dispute resolution options for all students. It includes no separate entitlement or due-process rights for most students with disabilities and their parents. It creates one system for all students that may include parental choice principles, with administrative remedies that are available for all students. It eliminates the current house-divided practices our schools face.

### DIRECTION 5: Celebrating the IDEA and reframing our efforts to create SPECIAL ED 2.0

In moving forward, this new law honors the success of the 1975 IDEA law, herein called "SPECIAL ED 1.0," and builds upon that through an honest national conversation to create a new twenty-first-century law—SPECIAL EDUCATION 2.0.

■ ■ ■

# Introduction

*Eleanor's story[2]*

*It is the first day of school in New York City some sixty years
ago—a bright and sunny early-September morning.
My friend's little sister, Eleanor, is six years old. Her mother takes her by the hand to walk to school.*

*However, at the schoolhouse door, they are prevented
from entering by the principal, who waves them away.
"We don't educate children like that," he insists.*

*Eleanor had Down syndrome, you see. She and her
mother returned home, and Eleanor never went to school.*

Stories like Eleanor's spurred advocacy efforts by parents and educators and, ultimately, court decisions that led in 1975 to passage of
the first national special-education law, the Individuals with Disabilities
Education Act (IDEA).[3] The IDEA was enacted in a different era. At that
time, about one million students with disabilities in the United States were
either not served at all or were poorly served by public schools. The law's
mission was to provide access to public education for all students with
disabilities. With this law, "Congress focused on eradicating an injustice
once and for all."[4] The law provided to students with disabilities access to
a free appropriate public education (FAPE) in the least restrictive environment (LRE). Briefly, a FAPE is an individualized program that is reasonably

calculated to provide the student with an educational benefit.[5] The law ended the exclusion of students with disabilities from public schools. Yet, in so doing, it has also been viewed as "impos[ing] its individual entitlement system on general education."[6]

Of course, the movement for access to education began long before 1975, driven primarily by parents and grassroots efforts awakening the nation to the injustice of exclusion. Several hard-fought pivotal lawsuits ensued and strengthened the push for a new law.[7]

Looking back over these forty-plus years, we can see that the IDEA succeeded in its mission. Now, all eligible students with disabilities—more than six million—have access to a FAPE in the LRE. These students make up some 13–14 percent of all students in US public schools.[8]

So, why not leave this successful program as is? Why fix it if it ain't broke? Unfortunately, it is "broke."

OK then, why not just fix the law we have? The answer is that we've tried that. Congress has tweaked the 1975 law in five hard-fought amendments and reauthorizations of the law.[9] But the law became ever more complex with more procedures, rights, and protections. It has left education neither sufficiently fluid nor effective for current times. A huge cottage—nay, "mansion"—industry of practitioners, advocates, lawyers, bureaucrats, and such, including me as a lawyer, has developed to serve and grow this law-induced activity.

We can trace the law's current challenges to Congress's approach of setting up an open-ended entitlement right for a specific (though imprecise and often subjectively defined) group—in this case, eligible students with disabilities and their parents. When the law was enacted in the 1970s civil-rights era, courts were used to solving society's challenges, and new rights and procedural protections were created. Twenty years later, Harvard Law School Professor Mary Ann Glendon, in *Rights Talk: The Impoverishment of Political Discourse,* wrote about the creation of rights and the new language of "rights talk" in America. This talk sets us apart from other countries by "its starkness and simplicity, its prodigality in bestowing the rights label, its legalistic character, its exaggerated absoluteness, its hyperindividualism, its insularity, and its silence with respect to personal, civic, and collective responsibilities."[10] Our system often appears to focus more on individual rights than on the common good.

Congress created this new, private enforcement system, tasking parents with the responsibility of enforcing their rights and the rights of their children. Not surprisingly and rather predictably, those rights have continued to grow and become, some say, "almost like reverse discrimination against the average kid."[11] No other group of students and parents, such as English-language learners, [12] gifted and talented, average, at risk, or any other group has an individual federal entitlement for education procedures or services. Indeed, "The IDEA is unusual…in that it creates individually enforceable rights to services."[13]

Along the way, this law created a quagmire of unintended consequences: rampant fear of litigation; too much bureaucratic regulation, paperwork, and cost; and input-driven requirements far removed from improving outcomes for students. The law's fairness and effectiveness are open to question.[14] Yet we kept on keeping on.

The evolution of the special-education law—from its great and just idea and hope to today's quagmires and dysfunction—is not unusual. Laws often morph and expand beyond their purpose, creating stakeholders who work to maintain the status quo. Anthony Lewis, a *New York Times* reporter and columnist, told of Supreme Court Justice Hugo L. Black, who thought that all government departments and agencies should be abolished every five or ten years, "Black…knew just about everything there was to know about how government works. His startling idea—and I think he was serious—was his solution for dealing with the encrustations of bureaucracy.[15]

At the time of this writing, Congress is expected to reauthorize the IDEA once again. Advocacy groups and stakeholders will promote their special interests. Congress will amend this and that, change discipline policies yet again, add or subtract assessments, reemphasize inclusion, and perhaps even allocate more resources. But inevitably Congress's tweaks and compromises will result in a reauthorizing of the same old law—another good-faith, cobbled-together stop-gap measure that responds to 1970s practices instead of twenty-first-century realities.

To paraphrase the *Wizard of Oz*'s Dorothy, "We are not in the 1970s anymore!" Tinkering will not get us to what we need today.

We know that education is our country's greatest equalizer and catalyst for growth and upward mobility. How best to do it now? For special education, it is clear that trying to effect positive systemic change by retrofitting an outdated law is not the way forward. We can't just keep on keeping on with the old broken system. This twentieth-century law simply doesn't fit the twenty-first century. We need to build a new law from the ground up.

So what is stopping us? What's driving us to stay with the old?

Dave's challenge led me down a new path. Before our café discussion, I had worked to fix the old IDEA.[16] Dave inspired me to create a new paradigm and law, keeping what was good and envisioning an effective new system for all children. This new law is SPECIAL ED 2.0.

This new law will be built on the foundation of the old law's success. It retains what's working, especially the fact that schools now educate all students with disabilities. Compare early telephones to the latest smartphone, or even to the first digital touch-screen phone that Apple introduced in 2007. How different they are! Smartphones have undergone many updates, each built on the successes and challenges of earlier ones and each introduced with a new number. So, too, here. It's time for special education's 2.0.

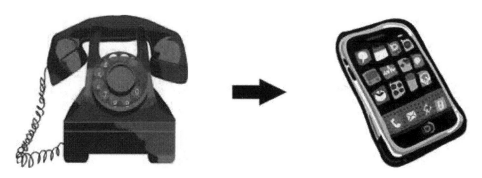

The dream: to have a national conversation to dream BIG and build a system that

- Educates *all* children with what they need to improve their lives and the future of our great country,
- Focuses on outcomes through research-based methods that work,

- Empowers teachers and parents as children's first teachers,
- Puts teachers at the helm and gets bureaucrats and lawyers out of classrooms and,
- Builds an effective, excellent, and equitable public schools system for all students, where all will truly mean *all!*

Undoubtedly it will be a long conversation toward a paradigm shift that will effectively and equitably lead us to educate all children. Change is hard. However, one thing is certain. It can't happen if we continue to be unable or unwilling to talk openly about the current situation. The IDEA, as we have known it, has taken us as far as it can. It is broken. Without delay, let's stop ignoring that "elephant in the room" and build a reality-driven twenty-first-century system.

When we stop putting off a challenge and start to act, often a surprising new world of opportunity awaits. I believe that will happen here. So, let's start this adventure together. Let's be bold. Education is optimism personified! Let's create a *new* law to educate *all* students.

# Part 1:  A brief history of special education and current reality

Special education is set up as a federal-funding statute for states that choose to participate and agree to comply with its requirements. These requirements include the provision of a free appropriate public education (FAPE) in the least restrictive environment (LRE) for students with disabilities. All states now participate.

When the law was enacted in 1975, the federal government authorized funding up to "40 percent of the average per-pupil expenditure" for educating students with disabilities.[17] That 40 percent target is called "full funding." But, the law turned out to be very costly for states and schools, as the federal dollars initially promised never materialized. The closest they came was in 2009 with the "stimulus package," the American Recovery and Reinvestment Act, when the federal government contributed 33 percent of the average per-pupil expenditure for one year. The average federal contribution has ranged between 8 percent and 18 percent per year since 1975. In 2014, it was 14 percent of average per-pupil cost.[18]

Initially designed to serve 10 percent of students, the IDEA now serves between 13 and 14 percent nationwide, with eligibility discrepancies among states ranging between 9 percent and 18 percent of students.[19] The law includes an individual entitlement for students with disabilities and their parents, relying on parents to enforce its "private enforcement system." It is a procedural, rights- and input-driven mechanism for developing individualized programs for students with disabilities; these programs are called Individualized Education Programs (IEPs). School personnel are charged with identifying students, evaluating them to determine their eligibility based on the law's criteria for services, and, if they are eligible, developing IEPs for them at local school-based team meetings. Such IEPs are to be reviewed and updated at least annually.

At all steps, parents are entitled to participate in the development of the IEP and to receive notice of the school's action (or lack of action). Parents have the right to consent to or reject services, evaluations, and other aspects of the process, and ultimately, if they dispute the school's action, to enforce the law through a dispute-resolution process that includes the right to mediation and due-process hearings. Due-process issues are about a host of issues, including student evaluation, eligibility for special education, placements, FAPE, services, attorneys' fees (which involve about half of all court decisions), and others. While schools also can seek due process, as a practical matter claims are most often brought by parents (approximately 85 percent of the time).[20]

Of note, the above IDEA description is written in the present tense because its structure, mandate, and entitlement have remained largely unchanged for more than forty years. It's still the same process-driven, complex entitlement that Congress enacted more than forty years ago, in 1975.

## The IDEA's current numbers and status

Today, of fifty-five million students in US public schools, some 6.4 million students with disabilities (13–14 percent of students age three to twenty-one) have been found eligible for services under current special-education law. Notably, during the period from 1985 to 2005, the number of general-education students grew by 20 percent, while the number of special-education students grew by 37 percent.[21] That disparity in growth has continued.

It was right and noble to end exclusions and discrimination. The 1975 law was a paradigm shift, changing our vision and education practices. How so? It was trailblazing; schools now educate all students. Even our language changed. The days of the terms "educable" and "noneducable" are but a distant memory. The current mantra is "All children can learn," even as the meaning of this phrase remains controversial.[22] Our nation leaped forward. Today many students with disabilities succeed in school, graduate from high school, go to college, and lead productive lives. The law forever changed how schools include and educate students with disabilities. It is right to toast its impact and success.[23]

# President Ford's Signing Statement for the IDEA

To round out this brief history and summary, President Gerald R. Ford's signing statement in 1975 is notable. While agreeing that the nation needed to do something about the fact that many children with disabilities, like Eleanor, were denied access to education, he was not convinced that the new law would do what its supporters hoped for.[24] Here is his December 2, 1975, Signing Statement for the Education for All Handicapped Children Act (IDEA's precursor):

> Unfortunately, this bill promises more than the Federal Government can deliver, and its good intentions could be thwarted by the many unwise provisions it contains. Everyone can agree with the objective stated in the title of this bill—educating all handicapped children in our Nation...
>
> Even the strongest supporters of this measure know as well as I that they are falsely raising the expectations of the groups affected by claiming authorization levels which are excessive and unrealistic.
>
> Despite my strong support for full educational opportunities for our handicapped children, the funding levels proposed in this bill will simply not be possible if Federal expenditures are to be brought under control and a balanced budget achieved over the next few years.

*There are other features in the bill which I believe to be objectionable and which should be changed. It contains a vast array of detailed, complex, and costly administrative require- ments which would unnecessarily assert Federal control over traditional State and local government functions. It establishes complex requirements under which tax dollars would be used to support administrative paperwork and not educational pro- grams. Unfortunately, these requirements will remain in ef- fect even though the Congress appropriates far less than the amounts contemplated in S. 6...*

*Fortunately since the provisions of this bill will not become fully effective until fiscal year 1978, there is time to revise the leg- islation and come up with a program that is effective and realistic. I will work with the Congress to use this time to design a program which will recognize the proper Federal role in helping States and localities fulfill their responsibilities in educating handicapped chil- dren. The Administration will send amendments to the Congress that will accomplish this purpose.[25]*

Ford was prescient in predicting today's challenges: the good intentions that raise hopes for unrealistic funding levels and the vast array of "de- tailed, complex, and costly administrative requirements" that support pa- perwork but not classroom work. The president hoped that, since the law would not become fully effective for three years, Congress could "revise the legislation and come up with a program that is effective and realistic."

Congress never did. It is left for us to help it do so.

## Under the IDEA, who is considered disabled? What is a disability?

Finding a student to be disabled and thus eligible for special-education services is a job reserved for the child's school-based IEP team. The team is made up of educators, other school personnel, parents, and others who may provide insight and information about the child.[26]

In 1975, following the medical model developed in prerevolutionary France for classifying disabilities, the law specified eight categories of students with disabilities.[27] Today, that number has expanded to thirteen and includes:

- Autism
- Deaf/blindness
- Deafness
- Emotional disturbance
- Hearing impairment
- Intellectual disability[28]
- Multiple disabilities
- Orthopedic impairment
- Other health impairment (OHI), including attention deficit disorder and attention-deficit/hyperactivity disorder (ADHD)
- Specific learning disability (SLD), sometimes called learning disability (LD)
- Speech or language (S/L) impairment

- Traumatic brain injury (TBI)
- Visual impairment, including blindness

Besides the increase in numbers of students and categories covered in the United States, another relevant difference between 1975 and today is that the law now largely serves a different group of students. Initially the law was designed for students with severe and profound mental and physical disabilities, such as intellectual disability, blindness, deafness, or multiple disabilities. Today that group makes up a minority of students with disabilities—estimated at 10–20 percent, depending on how students are classified.[29] Wade F. Horn and Douglas Tynan describe the number of students with disabilities,

> *Although the federal program was initially intended to address the educational needs of the severely disabled, today approximately 90 percent of special education students have lesser disabilities, such as a specific learning disability, speech and language delays, mild mental retardation, or an emotional disorder.*[30]

The vast majority (80–90 percent) of today's students with disabilities have mild or moderate needs, including specific learning disabilities (SLD), speech-language impairments, attention-deficit/hyperactivity disorder, other health impairments, and mild to moderate autism.

Forty to 50 percent of students with disabilities have the SLD designation. Estimates are that about 80 percent of these students are so labeled because they have not yet learned to read.[31]

Here is a chart of prevalence of disability categories in students age six to twenty-one in 2008. Information for the chart is from the National Center on Educational Outcomes.[32]

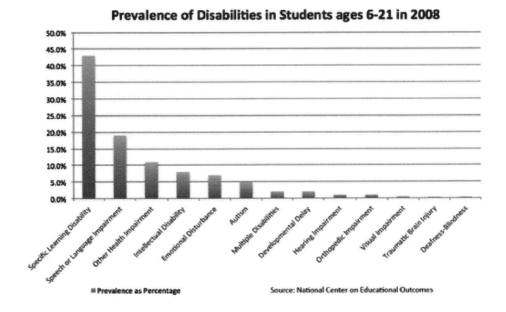

**Prevalence of Disabilities in Students ages 6-21 in 2008**

■ Prevalence as Percentage          Source: National Center on Educational Outcomes

The growth in the number of students identified with specific learning disorders (SLD) has been remarkable—a 300 percent rise between 1976 and 2000. Since 2002, there has been a modest annual decline of almost 2 percent, according to the National Center on Learning Disabilities. Government data for 2015 pegs specific learning disabilities (SLD) at 35 percent of the total number of students with disabilities—still by far the largest disability category.[33]

Current law requires students to have a diagnosis before they can be served, a reality that is problematic for several reasons and create quandaries for educators and parents alike. Membership in this designated group of students is imprecise. Unlike other programs whose membership parameters are clear and verifiable—those for veterans, seniors, and people in poverty, for example—this SLD group is often not measurable because the "diagnosis" is based on subjective and imprecise "criteria."[34]

Often it is impossible to tell the difference between students who are labeled as SLD and those who are not. In *Rethinking Special Education*, G. Reid Lyon and colleagues write,

> *Given what is now known about LD [herein, SLD], it is irresponsible to continue current policies that dictate inadequate identification practices...[F]rom its inception as a category, LD has served as a sociological sponge that attempts to wipe up general education's spills and cleanse its ills...There are few areas where the relationship of science and policy are more loosely linked than LD.[35]*

An *Education Week* online op-ed by a former principal discusses the fact that the current system leaves many students behind—simply because they have no diagnosis. He describes the "crack" kids who "are in the crack that contains students who can't keep up with their classmates, but aren't disabled enough to qualify for significant additional help."[36] One group is found eligible and entitled to individualized services, while the other far larger group—which includes many strugglers, "at-risk" students, and English-language learners, as well as those who are average or advanced—isn't eligible and is not entitled to individualized services.

For many students, their designation as SLD depends on the advocacy of teachers and parents or, alas, their zip code. For many others, no grownup is there to open a closed gate. The system still follows the old nineteenth-century medical model that requires students to be diagnosed to be served. Evaluators are the gatekeepers. Labels still rule.

The overall rise in SLD may be attributable as much to the law's "wait-to-fail" model as to the characteristics in children themselves. In real-world classrooms, the law still operates as a wait-to-fail model, labeling students only *after* they need services—in many cases, *after* they fail to learn appropriately in school for several years. The wait-to-fail model renders the law ineffective for many students. Services come too late. Instead of intervening when a child starts to struggle and have difficulty, which is *in fact* the research-based approach, too often the law provides catch-up services later.

The wait-to-fail model also sets up perverse incentives for parents and teachers. To meet the law's eligibility criteria, they have to focus *only* on a child's weaknesses and challenges to make him or her appear needier. The challenge appears to be global. A 2014 story quoted a parent in Ireland who fumed, "You are hoping for a worse diagnosis when the child is going to school. It's terrible."[37]

> *Why don't we teach students with mild and moderate learning and other disabilities without need for labels? What an indictment of this system of good intentions. Why do we keep it? Who is well served by it?*

# Provisions of the current IDEA

So what does the IDEA provide for students who are identified as disabled and their parents? First and foremost, the law guarantees a FAPE (a free appropriate public education) in the LRE (least-restrictive environment) to every eligible student with a disability between the ages of three and twenty-one. The FAPE is to be provided through an Individualized Education Program (IEP) that is designed to ensure that the student receives an educational benefit through specialized instruction that meets his or her unique needs.

Here is a summary of the specific rights and procedures:

**Referral and evaluation.** Children who may need special education are referred for an evaluation. Schools are also obligated to screen students to "find" students with disabilities.

**IEP team.** Thereafter, the IEP team (made up of educators, administrators, parents, and others) considers whether the student is eligible for special-education services.

**IEP.** If the student is eligible, he or she is entitled to an IEP (Individualized Education Program) that provides an FAPE.

**IEE.** Parents may be entitled to an IEE (Independent Educational Evaluation) of their child at school expense if they dispute the school's evaluation.

**Individualized services.** An IEP is an entitlement. Thus, if the IEP team includes specific services or placement on the IEP, those services must be provided, regardless of availability, costs, school budgets, and so forth.[38]

Through the law's private enforcement system, parents have the right (and challenge) to request the above procedures and programs and to enforce that right, including at hearings and in the courts.[39]

# The entitlement—its reach and effects

### Beth's story

*My young friend Beth's son was ready for kindergarten. His preschool experiences had been troubling, and he was suspended several times. Beth approached his entry into public school with trepidation, as she had been told by her friends and others that it would be hard to get services for her son.*

*So, several months before he set foot in the school and before she ever saw the program or met any of the teachers, Beth hired a lawyer!*

*You may ask, "Why?" Beth had been advised that she would have to fight the school for services.*

*Whither trust? What about the expectation that teachers are professional and work hard to meet student needs? How sad is all of this!*

*Yet, this is the system we've had for more than forty years.*

The IDEA sets up an *adversarial private enforcement system* to enforce the rights that it created. Parents act as "attorneys general" on behalf of themselves and their children. The law establishes extensive parental rights, including the right to participate in, consent to, reject, or dispute services offered by the school, even *before* they are provided. In looking back, among the law's many flaws (that, undoubtedly, some would call blessings) is this preemptive approach whereby parents can stop schools from implementing programs, even before they start.

As many of us see it now, the system has turned problematic as the opinions of people outside the school (lawyers, evaluators, parents, "experts," even judges) often hold sway over what takes place in classrooms with teachers who are, we can presume, the actual experts.

Let's be very clear: Parents did not create this system—they just want to help their children. Instead, it's the system that created the parents' need to fight. It's the system that is dysfunctional and broken.

This preemptive approach differs from other arenas in our lives. While we vet other professionals (doctors, lawyers, plumbers, and yes, veterinarians) before hiring them, we don't threaten to sue them before they do the work on the mere possibility that they might mess up. Think about the plumber who comes to unclog a sink. Can I sue (or threaten to sue) even before he starts the work?

What plumber would take that job? What teacher should take this job? Notably, forty-nine states now have teacher shortages—specifically, special-education teachers.[40]

> *It's time for an open and honest national conversation. Does providing for the threat of being sued, as the IDEA does, create good public policy and build trust between school and home? Is that the way we choose to move forward?*

The threat and fear of litigation in special education clouds relationships and effective practices. This "private enforcement" system has been called the IDEA's "structural design flaw,"[41] as it requires parents to wear three often ill-fitting and uncomfortable hats: first, consumers of government services; second, enforcers of government-derived rights; and third (and most important), carrying out their parental responsibilities while also partaking in the enjoyment of their children. Tasking parents with enforcing their own rights and their children's rights is most challenging.

## My immigrant mother's story

*My mother, brother, and I immigrated to the United States when I was in fourth grade. My mother was then, in today's parlance, a "single mom."*

*Though she was an educated middle-class woman, she was always reluctant to go to school to ask for ANYTHING! And she never did. While I would have benefited from changes in my education, there was NO WAY that she would make any demand or even a request of the New Jersey public school I attended. To her, educators were the experts, and she saw herself as a grateful parent. She just could not and would not question school authorities.*

Even today, my mother's long-ago story rings true for many immigrant, poor, or struggling parents. They may be afraid or reluctant to make any demand. Some, including parents who may be here illegally, are even at risk of deportation. Let's get real.

Added to the above, what is also very troubling is that, while it's fine for parents to advocate for their children (when they feel able to do so), the broader message should be one of encouraging parents and schools to collaborate for students—not impose a climate of threats, division, and intimidation. Teachers did not enter their profession in order to become witnesses at hearings—nor did parents become parents to do so.

In *Rethinking Special Education*, Tyce Palmaffy noted that advocates for the disabled "worry about the regulatory burden being placed on parents" by the law,

> In a scathing indictment of federal enforcement efforts that was issued in January 2000, the National Council on Disability wrote, "Enforcement of the law is too often the burden of parents who must invoke formal complaint procedures and request due process hearings to obtain the services and supports to which their children are entitled under law." There is a powerful minority of parents who know their legal rights and aren't afraid to exercise them. But most parents are at a decided disadvantage vis-à-vis school administrators. They don't know their rights, have little experience with the legal system, and tend to respect the decisions of professional educators.[42]

As discussed above, expecting parents to advocate *for* their children *against* the school is a nonstarter for many. The system leads to inequitable results, even within the students-with-disabilities community. The law embodies the "squeaky wheel" phenomenon: Those who can play (usually savvy, upscale parents who may even make excessive demands) "win," while many others—often poor, immigrant, and uneducated parents—"lose," leaving them and their children out.

Beyond this systemic dysfunction, this legal setup is flawed in other ways. First, the design flaw binds the states' and educators' hands. Waiting for and responding to parental consent interferes with their right (and responsibility) to educate all students in a timely manner. Second, while parents may be experts about their children at home, they are neither professionals nor educational experts at school. Third, at its troubling core, this adversarial system is built on the premise that parents and schools are *not* on the same page, working cooperatively for the benefit of children. Fourth, this system kills trust. Trust, the bedrock for any good relationship, is too often thwarted by this law—as shocking as that is—that fosters division between school and home. It presumes that parents and students need "protections" *from* their schools and need to advocate *for* their children *against* their schools. Just think about that language!

The good news is that, overwhelmingly, various state and district-wide surveys show that most parents of children with disabilities appear satisfied with their children's education.[43] Yet, this general satisfaction is often overshadowed by a relatively small number of due-process disputes that generate great costs in time and resources for schools, educators, and parents alike.

The number of actual hearing decisions is low and generally declining. Of over six million students with disabilities in the United States, 2,262 decisions were rendered in 2011–12, compared with 4,537 in 2006-07. Further, 94–96 percent of cases that start down the due-process path end up being settled or withdrawn.[44] A mere trickle of a trickle![45]

While the small number of hearing decisions may be a good thing, it is also a mixed blessing in several ways. First, the effect of this small number of disputes is huge as the fear of litigation and government findings of noncompliance with regulations permeates schools. Second, the cost of settlements, often in the form of cost-sharing programs between parents and schools—adds further budgetary pressures on school.[46] And third, this adversarial system has turned "professional development" for teachers and administrators into sessions about legal and bureaucratic requirements—training school personnel about how to dot all i's and cross all t's on paperwork and compliance rather than how to improve education practice.[47]

Congress attempted to respond to these challenges by creating two pilot projects to reduce paperwork and regulations through waivers. But, surprise, surprise, there were *no* takers among schools anywhere! How can that be? The US Government Accountability Office (GAO) recently reported,

> *The National Association of Secondary School Principals told us that none of their members were in favor of the paperwork waivers, in part because of the perceived risk of exposing local districts to potential litigation if they were to eliminate any of the requirements that parents have come to expect.*[48]

You can't make this stuff up.

In short, the IDEA's entitlement, built on an adversarial due-process system, has led to an emphasis on litigation, not learning; has put schools on the defensive and questioned the expertise of their professionals; and has confused and angered parents.

### *My story*

I'll never forget when the power of this law hit home. It was precipitated by a meeting with my son's high-school principal one evening. He held once-a-month meetings with an open door—no appointment needed. I went to discuss my concerns. The principal listened politely and then ended the conversation with, "Thank you for coming in, Ms. Freedman. Have a great evening."

Before I got up to leave, I asked, "Would you dismiss me quite so fast if I were a parent of a student with a disability? Wouldn't you tell me that you'll look into my concerns and contact the special education department about my concerns?

The principal smiled sheepishly. He understood.

While Congress may have thought (and hoped) that it had created a collaborative and positive system, folks in the field and parents will tell you that it did not. Too often, the system is brutal and adversarial. [49]

> *Let's step away to ask a BIG question: Would anyone seeking to create a positive, collaborative system for teachers, parents, and students set up the adversarial, bureaucratic, and trust-killing system that we have?*

## Funding and data collection for this uncapped entitlement leads to resource inequality

The IDEA imposes *no* caps on time, money, or effort for the protected groups (students with disabilities and their parents), which leads to funding and data collection distortions and resource inequality for all students.

How can this happen? We hardly know, because surprisingly—actually, shockingly—the federal government does not collect data about the costs for special education and the costs for educating students with disabilities. Indeed, a 2011 Fordham Institute study, *Shifting Trends in Special Education*, reported as "scandalous" the fact that we still do not know how much is spent to educate these students.

> *Yet we know precious little about how this money is spent at the state or district level. Indeed, state special-education expenditures are not easy to obtain; states are not required to report these data to the federal government, and few volunteer to disentangle their special-education expenditures from their reported general-education expenditures...Accurate accounting of state, district, and school-level spending on special education simply does not exist...In a time of tight resources—and special-education expenditures surpassing $110 billion per annum—there's an increasing need for reliable financial data at all levels. That such large swaths*

*of state and district budgets can go essentially unmeasured and unreported is scandalous...We can no longer view these as untouchable expenditures.*[50]

Given this lack of data, this discussion is limited to cost *estimates*. Funding for special education and the education of students with disabilities comes from three major sources: local, state, and federal dollars. Since the federal government has never come close to "full funding" special education, local and state taxes have been called upon to make up the difference—often a painful stretch.[51] Students with disabilities receive services, no matter their local school district's budget, while services for other students may be encroached upon. "Encroachment" happens when a mandated open-ended entitlement takes resources from other programs. The phenomenon causes confusion and consternation. Special education can (and often does) distort schools' resource allocation, usurping the education needs of all students. [52]

The costs for special education and for educating students with disabilities are not the same. One is included within the other, as this chart demonstrates.[53]

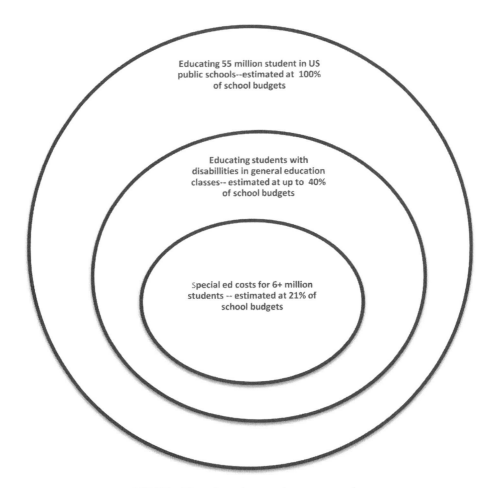

NOTE: The chart is not drawn to scale.

The total expenditure for public education (K-12) in 2012–13 was $620 billion (or $12,296 per student enrolled in the fall of 2012).[54]

"Special-education costs" cover specialized instruction, evaluators, private placements, personnel, equipment, buildings, and other services provided to a student through an IEP, while the costs for "educating students with disabilities" also includes the services that these students receive in general-education classrooms—a large component, as most students with disabilities spend most of their day in inclusive or mainstream settings.[55]

The Fordham Institute study cited above found that the cost of special education consumed 21 percent of school budgets. In 2005, it cost "a whopping $110 billion that year alone…[and] we know precious little about how this money is spent at the state and district level."[56]

We also do not know how much it costs to educate students with disabilities—a higher number, as that cost combines the special and general-education services they receive.  One 2009 study in California stated, "Special education spending doesn't cover the regular education costs of educating students with disability."[57] It's been estimated that the cost approaches 40% of school budgets.  Sadly, we just don't know.

Special education has become a huge "industry" in all states. Its costs and the cost of educating students with disabilities continue to rise. Between 1996 and 2005, an estimated 40 percent of all new public-education dollars went to special-education services.[58]

Special education is a principal driver of public-school spending, and its bureaucratic and programmatic mandates reach into every corner of our public schools. In fact, it distorts the purpose of our schools because *everyone* should have a right to an appropriate share of resources. Students may be harmed when funds are taken for this one entitlement program.[59] The lack of hard cost data is troubling. While Congress requires states and schools to provide extensive data about students with disabilities, it does *not* require cost data. Urgently, it should. We can't begin to manage this behemoth without knowing its parameters.

## Comparison to other student groups— funding and data collection

**W**hat about other students, such as gifted and talented, to use the federal government's terminology? These students are also called advanced or high-potential students.

Reportedly, the US spends 143 times as much for students with disabilities as it does for gifted and talented students![60] A shocking statistic, as I see it.

The Jacob K. Javits Gifted and Talented (G & T) Student Education Program is the sole federal-funding source for gifted and talented students. It identifies and serves students who are traditionally underrepresented in G & T programs, including minority or low-income students, English-language learners, and students with disabilities.[61] In 2015, the Javits Program received a $10 million appropriation. In some years, Congress provides no appropriation for this Program.

In 2014, the *Education Week Blog* reported that Congress authorized funding for the Javits program at $5 million and for special education, at $11.5 billion.[62] Amazing, isn't it?

Read on. It gets more lopsided.

While gifted and talented students make up some 6 percent of students, programs for them receive just 1 percent of school budgets in federal, state, and local funds.[63] In contrast, students with disabilities (13–14 percent of students) receive an estimated 21–40 percent.

Is this wide discrepancy a smart public policy? Not as I see it, for many reasons. First, it is dangerous to our long-term national interest.

Our students now compete in an interconnected and competitive world. International test scores show that our most advanced students are falling behind their international peers: "Top US students are falling behind even average students in Asia."[64]

Second, it is unfair, inequitable, and seriously out of balance when the perceived needs of a small group overwhelm the needs of most students. How can that possibly be fair—or sustainable? Stanford professor Mark Kelman writes,

> We should scrutinize all claims that non-disabled students face disruption...But we should be equally wary of a system that forbids us from counting the educational interests of "mainstream" students just as worthy as those of pupils with disabilities.
>
> In a world of limited resources, it is plainly not enough to say that children with learning disabilities "deserve" more resources; their claims inevitably compete with claims that could be made for other "deserving" pupils who can be described in a wide variety of ways (such as poor achievers, socioeconomically disadvantaged, and gifted but under stimulated).
>
> Until we see that these are important education issues but not civil rights claims, we will not make rational policy in this area.[65]

It has never been made clear why *only* students with disabilities still need such "protections" after forty-plus years of successfully gaining access to education. Specifically for students with learning disabilities, the question of why they "are more deserving of extra help than everyday low achievers is one that [their] advocates have never quite answered."[66]

About data collection, the federal government collects vast amounts of data about special education. The *36th Annual Report to Congress on the Implementation of the Individuals with Disabilities Education Act, 2014* by the Office of Special Education and Rehabilitative Services (OSERS) of the US Department of Education (DOE) presents 289 pages of data and analysis, with many additional links to other data used in preparing that report.[67] And Congress mandates such detailed reports yearly.

What data are schools required to collect (or is collected) about other student groups? Actually, data about non-English-language speakers, gifted and talented, bored, advanced, slow, dreamers, "at risk," socially maladjusted, poor, rich, and other groups are either not collected or, when collected, are far less detailed or extensive.[68]

If it is true, as a Gates Foundation website post states, "We care about what we measure, and measure what we care about," then this imbalance is truly troubling.[69]

Specifically, the National Association for Gifted Children reports that the US government collects *no* data about the three to five million gifted and talented students in grades K-12.[70]

Why might this be? Some say that gifted and talented students don't need programs as they will take care of themselves, and it is elitist to focus on them. The conventional wisdom is that our top students are doing just fine, even as current testing results show that they also don't meet their potential. As well, often overlooked are the unmet social and emotional issues of gifted and talented students.[71]

Others may argue that the answer is to give all students an individual entitlement: "Give everyone an IEP!" I disagree. The notion that we would want educators to become ever more mired in paperwork, meetings, and additional rights to "protect" students from schools makes me cringe. Were we to do that, we might as well hand our schools over to bureaucrats and lawyers more than we already have, kissing teaching and learning goodbye. I write as an attorney—expressing a position that is clearly against pocketbook interests. More regulations, paperwork, and "rights" do *not* improve education. More time in class spent on teaching and learning does.

The answer is obvious. To end the imbalance among groups, we need to focus on and pay attention to *all* groups and end the individual entitlement for a single group. All students need appropriate services and the opportunity to achieve excellence.

Even Congress seems to agree. Since enacting the IDEA in 1975, it has created *no* additional individual educational entitlement program.[72] In 2015, when signing the Every Student Succeeds Act (ESSA), former President Obama spoke of the American *ideal*, not *individual entitlement* that every child should have: "With this bill, we reaffirm that fundamentally American *ideal*—that every child, regardless of race, income, background, the zip code where they live, *deserves the chance* to make of their lives what they will."[73]

## Nagging questions about the program's effectiveness

**B**eyond these huge sums of public funds, where is evidence of the payoff, of good—dare we ask for great?—results? Consider this from the Spring 2009, issue of *CommonWealth Magazine*, "The cost of special education in Massachusetts is approaching $2 billion a year...There is little evidence that the state's...investment is paying off as hoped."[74] We have no evidence that the law's procedures, requirements, litigation, and fear of litigation improve educational outcomes for children. None.

> *Current entitlement, inequitable funding and data collection, and inconclusive outcomes continue. We are left to ask BIG questions:*
>
> *Who is invested in the status quo and who is hurt by it? Why can't we move the needle toward equitable and effective programs?*

# Part 2: Six impediments that stop change

**W**hat gets in the way of change? If you believe, as I do, that we can do better for our students and nation, let's explore this question. What impediments do we face?

# The first impediment— many provisions of law, regulations, federal and state directives lack objective research

## The principal's story

I recently spoke with an elementary school principal. He was a kind, soft-spoken man, proud to share that his is an "inclusive school." I asked if he knew of any research about inclusion from the perspective of general-education students. He did not. What he had was anecdotes—many that touch the heart.

When asked if general-education teachers or parents of general-education students complain that inclusion is not working for them, he said that they do. But, and this shocked me, he tells parents who don't like it that they can pull their kids out and send them to private school!

I asked an obvious follow-up question: Is he putting the interests of students with disabilities ahead of others? He acknowledged that perhaps he is, saying that we have to educate all students. That left me speechless, wondering if he appreciated the irony of what he had said. Which students are "all" students?

There it is—inclusion in one elementary school. I wonder how common this principal's attitude is.

Take, for example, the current push for "mainstreaming" or "inclusion," which the law calls the "least restrictive environment" (LRE). "Inclusion refers to the practice of students with disabilities learning alongside their peers in general-education classrooms."[75] The movement is powerful and ever-present; its graphics are inviting and often heartwarming.76

However, it is important to take a step back and remember that inclusion is *not* a legal mandate. The word does not appear in the law. Instead, the LRE (least restrictive environment), a phrase that *does* appear in the law, is a "strong Congressional *preference*" to have students with disabilities educated with their nondisabled peers "to the maximum extent *appropriate*" to *meet the child's unique needs.*[77] Note that the LRE requirement focuses on the student with the IEP, not on his or her classmates. Further, schools and parents have been embroiled in years of litigation trying to define the term "appropriate" and the level of benefit that it entails. Even after forty years of policy directives and litigation, the meaning of "appropriate" in the description of LRE and in the phrase "free appropriate public education" (FAPE) remains in dispute—and, in fact, is currently before the Supreme Court again.[78]

What does it mean for students with disabilities or for their general-education peers?

As for general-education students, the short answer is that we don't know. Their perspective and needs have not generally been considered in the movement toward inclusion. Inclusion is largely promoted by advocates for students with disabilities who argue that in order to learn and become self-sufficient those students need to be educated among nondisabled peers.[79] Surely these are good goals, so why is this concerning? Inclusion continues to be plagued by many unanswered concerns.

To start the inquiry, where is the supporting *objective* data, especially about inclusion's effects on *all* students in our nation's classrooms and on different groups of students with disabilities?

In many ways, inclusion grew out of the civil-rights movement, not out of pedagogy or research-supported practices. Following *Brown v. Board of Education of Topeka*, the landmark 1954 racial discrimination lawsuit, the notion of educating students with disabilities in regular schools entered public-school classrooms.[80] The Principals' Partnership stated, "According to the literature, inclusion is not a strategy, but a philosophy."[81]

In 2012, the American Institute for Research analyzed evidence about inclusive practices. Here are some findings:

> [A] positive association is shown for the percentage of students in special education spending 80 percent or more of their school day in general education classes in district-level analyses. [Source omitted.] This variable is of particular interest because it may be one of the best measures available of the extent to which students with disabilities (and all students) are receiving the social benefits associated with interacting with a diverse student

*enrollment. In addition, the data above suggest that some academic benefit for students with disabilities may be associated with this variable as well.*[82]

Is that the basis of this national push? An *apparent* benefit for students with disabilities and an *association* of one data point with another; social benefits that *may* accrue; a "may be" association of academic benefits for students with disabilities—and *silence for the majority of students?* Troubling questions remain, starting with the reality that a correlation does not equate to causation. Does the research provide more than a tentative foundation for the gospel of inclusion and mainstreaming in our nation's classrooms? Do we have reliable evidence that all students, including those in special and general education, benefit academically from inclusion? Are there proven social benefits for special and general-education students? What I've been able to glean has been unsettling, incomplete, and largely unpersuasive. It is troubling that research is often produced by researchers who approach the issues from the perspective of special education, and not from the perspective of all students.[83]

At the time this book was being edited, there was some reason for optimism, as researchers may be starting to consider the needs for all students. *Education Week* headlined a first-page story about "preliminary" research findings in this way, "Inclusive Classes Have Downsides..." The story focused on a specific segment of students—young general-education students who are placed in classes with students with emotional and behavioral disabilities. "[Y]oung children who shared a classroom with pupils who have emotional and behavioral disabilities had more absences, lower math and reading scores in kindergarten and 1st grades, and were more likely to act out in the classroom or struggle with social skills."

Those effects have been called "the spillover effects." The article went on to indicate that these effects "have not been widely explored."[84] Alas, that is so.

Needless to say, these issues and research are highly controversial. The story acknowledges that while "inclusion has long been a fundamental tenet of special education...actual research on the benefits of including students with such disabilities has been scarce over the past 10 years..."[85]

The bottom line is this. We need objective, empirical research—by nonpartisan researchers— to focus on the needs of all students.

Yet, finding such researchers in education is hard. Too often, data depends on who puts it forward and what "latest new thing" or panacea it promotes. A recent *Education Week* op-ed sought "edu-scholars" to "tell the truth." Imagine that—the need for truth and objective data![86] Clearly, the challenge reaches beyond (and includes) special education and the inclusion/mainstreaming movement.

This national movement reminds me of the fifty-plus-year anti-fat obsession—popular and driven by government programs—until it stopped in its tracks, proven wrong.

Started in the 1970s on the basis of research that turned out to be flawed, it took close to fifty years to finally unwind. In 2014, Nina Teicholz's *The Big FAT Surprise: Why Butter, Meat & Cheese Belong in a Healthy Diet,* uncovered the poor research  underpinning for the government's push—a policy that, sadly, may have led to the obesity and diabetes epidemics we now face. After the book came out in 2014, headlines blared: "Surprise, fat is good for you!" and "Everyone was wrong: Saturated fat can be good for you." And, from England, "Doctors change their minds after 40 years: Fat is good for you."[87]

So now, we're back to eating eggs and meat and it's sugar and carbs that are considered bad for you.

*A cautionary tale indeed.*

Yet, the inclusion beat goes on. In spite of an incomplete and often one-sided research basis, governments continue to pressure schools to advance inclusion per se, substituting the opinions of government officials for educators and parents who know the student. For example, Indicator 5, a metric established by OSERS, targets schools to have students with disabilities in general-education classes 80 percent of the time. Yet, what about what students' IEPs say or which settings actually are "appropriate" for them.[88]

Along with that *Education Week* op-ed, I urge researchers to study what works before government policies advance additional research-deprived policies on another generation of students.

> *Educators are left scratching their heads: Which law do you want us to obey? Is it the IDEA that requires individualization or government' current group-based inclusion directives? When did government become empowered to direct IEP teams about children's needs and services?*

Next, the research basis for and merits of the LRE remain controversial. Apparently, controversy exists also in England, where, about ten years ago, the BBC reported on a leading inclusion-policy architect who changed her mind. "She now believes that, although it may have been right at the time, inclusion has been taken 'too far,' driven by political correctness rather than a judgment of what is always best for the child."[89] In the United States, it's been generally taboo to raise issues about that, spawning a deafening silence among general educators, policymakers, and parents of general (and some special) education students. Quietly, some parents withdraw their children from school.

Also largely ignored are the views of specific groups *within* the disability community. In particular, many parents of students who are blind, deaf, hard of hearing, or have specific learning disabilities vigorously oppose inclusion. In discussing these various views, Thomas Hehir, a Harvard Graduate of Education professor, wrote, "The issue (inclusion) is so controversial within the [special-education] community that virtually every disability group has developed a position."[90] Where is the credible objective evidence that placing a student with disabilities who is several years behind his or her peers in a general-education classroom actually benefits that student's learning? Even without such evidence, the train to do just that has already left the station and keeps on rolling.

And what about the voices of general educators—obviously stakeholders in their own classrooms? Too often they are ignored or minimized. For example, recent special-education task forces in California and Washington State, which convened to study current practices and recommend reform, consisted mostly of members drawn from the special-education community—personnel and parents—not general education.[91]

Yet, these task forces recommend that services be implemented most often in general-education classrooms! How does state policy get general-education buy-in for the nation's 86 percent of students who are not defined as disabled by current law when their voices are underrepresented at the planning table? In my informal discussion with former US Secretary of Education John King, he was sympathetic to the notion that we need to bring general educators to the planning table.[92]

Too often the inclusion drive contorts the purpose of schooling, appearing to make inclusion the goal and applying approaches to make it "work." Now we speak of "inclusive schools," as the principal's story above demonstrated.

Surely, the notion that a school's mission is inclusion—not excellence, instruction, or learning—is worthy of a robust conversation among all stakeholders. What happens to academics, social skills, and learning for *all* students?

To make inclusion work, government and advocates push approaches whose research basis for all students are often unknown and remain controversial, especially on a large scale. These include the use of differentiated instruction; multi-tiered system of supports (MTSS); other interventions, accommodations and modifications; 1:1 aides; and others.[93]

For example, take *differentiation*, the currently popular theory whereby teachers are to use different approaches to teach the wide spectrum of learners in their classrooms, from the strugglers to the most advanced, and all those in between. Through differentiation, it is claimed, teachers can effectively teach all students in general-education classrooms, whatever their needs and current performance levels. This theory is advanced even as it remains controversial and data about its efficacy *for all students* either does not exist or is inconclusive.[94] Of course, in pockets of excellence, it can work. But, that would seem to be a circular argument. Doesn't everything work when done right? James R. Delisle concluded the *Education Week* discussion of differentiation with this, "I can conclude only one thing: Differentiation works...unless it doesn't."[95]

Given what we know, is it realistic to try to scale that as national policy for all students?

Finally, the drive for inclusion contradicts research showing the effectiveness of the opposite classroom structure, namely that educating students by current performance levels works well and improves student outcomes.[96] The current success of proficiency-based programs that group students with others at similar skill and knowledge levels—groupings that are flexible and change as students learn at their own pace—provides a hopeful sign that objective research can, in fact, drive effective programming. If we, as a nation, are still interested in improving student outcomes for all students, it is time to put the focus squarely on practices and approaches that actually work—not on philosophically appealing or "feel good" approaches.

Bruce Meredith and Julie Underwood, in their excellent 1995 analysis about the coming conflict between general and special education, explain how the basic paradigm issues between general and special education are structured—one (general education) focuses on the group, and one (special education) focuses on the individual. They conclude the following about meeting the needs of all students in inclusive classrooms: "Unfortunately, courts have largely ignored this issue precisely because its resolution is so difficult and politically sensitive."[97] That was twenty years ago. The situation is even more entrenched now.

> *How did our purpose get so turned around so that governments push inclusion in spite of lack of objective data for all students, while ignoring research on placements that actually work.*

> *Let's be clear! The argument here is not whether inclusion is good or bad. It is that we still don't know its effects on and effectiveness for all students. Dare we ask why we aren't even talking about that?*

## The second impediment—how standards are conveyed and discussed—often, the public is told one thing while reality is quite different

### *A concerned mother's story*

*Before joining my law firm, I was a Massachusetts hearing officer, hearing special-education cases.*

*One story has stayed with me for years—of a mother of a 7th grader with learning disabilities. At the child's first IEP team meeting at the junior high school, teachers shared their concerns about his lack of basic academic skills.*

*To which the mother responded, "But I don't understand. He got all A's and B's in elementary school!"*

*Indeed he did. Apparently teachers had modified and simplified his work and expectations, and passed him on the basis of those modified expectations without full parental notice.*

We need to stop lying to students, parents, and citizens about achievement, lest we become yet another Lake Wobegon, where "all the children are above average…"[98]

For example, consider these recent examples about graduation rates…and their meaning.

The federal government is focusing on improved graduation rates. States are falling in line and graduating more students, including students with disabilities.

Graduation rates for all students have risen over the past ten years to 82 percent in 2014—a good thing! Graduation rates for students with disabilities have also risen, but at lower rates, and they remain lower.[99] Government reports indicate that in 2006, 57 percent of these students graduated from high school with a diploma; another report shows that their graduation rate rose from 59 percent in 2011 to 63.1 percent in 2015.[100]

Yet, where is proficiency? The National Assessment of Educational Progress (NAEP) is often called "the nation's report card." It recently reported that scores disappoint again—not so good! According to the 2016 NAEP, fewer than 40 percent of high school graduates are career or college ready.[101] That means more than 60 percent are *not*. How this squares with the rising graduation rates discussed above is not clear.

An NPR (National Public Radio) broadcast, "The Truth about Graduation Rates," explored four explanations for the rise in graduation rates and concluded that graduation rates are "still highly subjective numbers, in spite of the attempt to track rates from state to state. In short, it's still not clear what a diploma means."[102] As well, a *New York Times* lead editorial, "The Counterfeit High School Diploma," discussed the fact that while more students graduate, they are *not* ready for college or the workforce.

*Nationally, graduation rates are rising—yet less than 40 percent of twelfth-graders are ready for math and reading at the college level. An alarming study by the Education Trust, a nonpartisan foundation, found that more than one in five recent high school graduates could not meet minimum entry tests to enlist in the Army.*[103]

In 2010, Michael Kirst, professor emeritus at Stanford University and president of the California Board of Education, estimated that 60 percent of students (including students with disabilities) in community colleges and 30 percent in four-year colleges need remedial courses in college.[104] Most of these unprepared students leave college before earning a credential.

Former US Secretary of Education Arne Duncan spoke at the annual NAACP conference in 2010, where he highlighted what he called "dummy standards" that lie to children, ...that tell children they are ready for college when they are not...we have to stop lying to children, to parents, and to ourselves...[105]

"Passing" grades may make students, teachers, administrators, and parents feel better—until they realize that, actually, students did not master the skills taught and tested. Graduating unprepared students is unfair and has serious consequences.

"Stop with the political correctness and just admit it—lots of high school graduates aren't ready for college," writes Michael J. Petrilli, president of the Thomas B. Fordham Institute.[106] Petrilli notes that the gap between college preparedness in reading and enrollment rates has been widening steadily since 1992 and that just 53 percent of all students who enroll in college graduate with a degree six years later.

## The third impediment—the use of language that leads us astray

Closely related to standards and graduation rates are the "honesty gap" and doublespeak. *Merriam-Webster* defines "doublespeak" as language that can be used in more than one way and is used to deceive people. The "honesty gap" is a term that has popped up in the testing-and-achievement arena. It refers to the gap between information that parents receive and how students are actually doing.[107] In special education, some oft-used terms that create a barrier to honest dialogue and trust—and impede our ability to understand a student's needs—include the following:

"Closing gaps" and "closing the gap." A great goal, perhaps, but what does it mean? How real is it? Concerns are raised when we lower or "dumb down" standards—bringing all to a "middling" level; provide invalidating modifications of standards; hurt advanced students who are already proficient (and beyond current federal testing policy's focus); and obsess about having all students go to college. This obsession ignores research about the benefits of vocational and technical education and non-academic careers, as well as the reality that many students are simply unprepared for college. One running joke is that we can "close achievement gaps" by simply ending achievement.

How about aiming to "narrow gaps"—a realistic and, frankly, more honest goal.

"We need to meet the needs of all students all the time." Let's be honest; we can't. One hundred percent is a meaningless target.[108]

"All students can learn and meet the same—or aligned—challenging academic standards." What does this actually mean? How real is it?

"We need challenging standards." Sure. But, what are they? What does *challenging* or *rigorous* mean?

Remember the No Child Left Behind Act's (NCLB) ambitious but impossible goal—that all students would be proficient on rigorous standards by 2014? Rather predictably, that did not happen. Instead, most states received waivers. The year 2014 and the NCLB law have come and gone (replaced in 2015 by ESSA) without achieving universal proficiency. Students still failed to learn what they needed. We as a nation muddled through, and faith in the system took a hit.

> *The "honesty gap" and doublespeak hurt efforts to rebuild trust and positive relationships among school, home, and community.*

## The fourth impediment—focusing on weaknesses—not the whole child's strengths as well as weaknesses

**"Do you like this child?"**

*Another memorable case from my days as a hearing officer was about a high-school student with low-average cognitive potential and multiple disabilities. Let's call him Sam. His mother's testimony detailed the challenges and difficulties he faced, supported by reports by evaluators that she read and quoted. In short, she explained all he things Sam could not do.*

*Finally, having heard so much about his weaknesses, I looked up and asked, "Do you like this child?"*

*She stopped and looked at me. Then she smiled. She got it—and proceeded to talk about Sam's strengths, giving those present at the hearing a more balanced picture of him.*

Current special-education law "endlessly splices and dices student weaknesses and diagnoses. The law mentions but does not emphasize student strengths. As a result, we have inadvertently created a generation of students with disabilities who focus on what they *cannot* do."[109]

Unfortunately, many students with disabilities have developed what is termed "learned helplessness."[110]

In contrast, in our daily lives most of us seem to know it's smart to focus on strengths and perseverance. Check out the bestsellers by Marcus Buckingham and Tom Rath, and, of course, the popular trailblazing work in Carol Dweck's *Mindset: The New Psychology of Success.*[111]

## The fifth impediment—burdensome regulations and compliance that force teachers to do *less* teaching and *more* paperwork

About compliance. Back in 2002, the *President's Commission on Excellence in Special Education* found more than 814 procedural monitoring requirements for compliance by state and local programs. It concluded that "educators spend more time on process compliance than on improving educational performance for children with disabilities..."[112] The situation has not improved over the past fourteen years.

I recently attended a special-education conference for teachers and administrators. Of eighty-six breakout sessions, 38 percent were about legal issues and compliance—presented by attorneys. Need we say more? *Lawyers don't teach; teachers do.* The endless requirements and red tape that bind teachers create obstacles to education practice and success. Litigation and the even more corrosive fear of litigation that drives the compliance beast impede the ability of teachers, administrators, and parents to prioritize needs and improve outcomes for all students, including students with disabilities.

"Red tape" is "official routine or procedure marked by excessive complexity which results in delay or inaction."[113] We are mired in it! Special-education teachers complain of the paperwork burdens imposed by this law. A January 2016 NPR report highlighted the fact that forty-nine states have a shortage of special-education teachers. Why? Many special-education teachers leave the field, far more than do general-education teachers.

Among the primary reasons for their departures are "the paperwork, the meetings, the accountability."[114]

The NPR report cites research by Professor Donald Deshler of the University of Kansas showing that special-education teachers spend only 27 percent of their time on instruction. The rest is spent on oversight of IEPs, meetings, co-teaching, and data management. Deshler says, "If we wonder why teachers are frustrated, this data sheds some light on it."[115]

It gets worse. Of the above-cited 27 percent of time spent teaching, only 21 percent was what Deshler considered "specialized instruction," meaning that teachers were using evidence-based methods focused on students' individual needs. "Twenty-one percent of their time is spent teaching the best of what we know. That roughly translates into one day a week," Deshler stated in the same article.

In 2014, amid great fanfare, in response to continuing and growing concerns about the compliance web, paperwork, and such, the US Department of Education (DOE) rolled out its Results-Driven Accountability (RDA) initiative to reduce compliance mandates. Unfortunately, from first reports, it seems that the RDA adds outcome efforts on top of the law's procedural requirements. For example, Massachusetts's description of RDA states that it is a way of "Insuring compliance *and* improving results."[116]. I heard Melody Musgrove, the former head of the Office of Special Education Programs (OSEP) at the time of the RDA rollout, assure (!) the audience that the department was not letting go of compliance.[117] It is not clear how and whether compliance will be de-emphasized, going forward.

Can it really be that, instead of its focus on compliance, the federal government *adds* improving results without *removing* compliance—expecting improved results? All in a six-plus hour day! Hmmm. How will that work?

As discussed above, in its 2004 reauthorization, Congress acknowledged the paperwork burdens and tried to reduce it through two pilot projects and waivers. Yet, according to the US Government Accountability Office's (GAO) 2016 report, there were *no* takers because it was too costly and risky to use those pilot projects![118] Besides the response by the National Association of Secondary Schools, described earlier, that it was too risky in terms of possible litigation, the National Association of Directors of Special Education stated that the waiver application required too much new paperwork and additional staffing.

Amazing. But is anyone surprised?

Finally, and most importantly, adding to this imbalance and, dare I say, outrage, we have *no* evidence showing that procedural compliance improves student outcomes. None.

*Why do we stay on this path—mired in twentieth-century thinking and law?*

In 2015, a very hopeful sign, Congress passed and former President Obama signed the Every Student Succeeds Act (ESSA). It is to be fully implemented by 2017, when the NCLB Act will become history. For general education, ESSA sends much authority over education back to the states and local school districts. As part of the national conversation proposed by SPECIAL ED 2.0, let us urge Congress to also ease the federal government's current bureaucratic and regulatory stranglehold over special education so that states and school districts are freed and can appropriately educate all students in their communities.

## The sixth impediment—current personnel-hiring practices in schools

The compliance focus affects school-personnel hiring. Fewer than half of school personnel are teachers. Many are hired to monitor and comply with federal and state requirements. Others may be administrators, clerical staff, lawyers, guidance counselors, social workers, or paraprofessionals. In 2006, while 43 percent of school personnel in the US were teachers, in other countries, that percentage was 70 to 80 percent. The Fordham Institute reports, "Non-teaching staff grew by 130 percent between 1970 and 2010, while student enrollment grew by 8.6 percent."[119] Too often the current system focuses on administrators and ancillary personnel in central offices and lawyers and judges in hearing or courtrooms, instead of teachers in our nation's classrooms. The emphasis seems to be on "doing it (procedures) right," not on "doing the right thing" for students.

## Conclusion about current law and practice— and changed priorities ahead!

First, this is the story of mission accomplished! In many ways, the IDEA is an American success story. It now provides access to appropriate education for all students with disabilities. No one is excluded—a great achievement, indeed. Initially planned for 10 percent of students, the law now serves 13–14 percent. Initially planned for eight categories of disabilities, it now serves thirteen. Let's be very clear: As we move to build a new law on the foundation of the old one, with all students who have disabilities receiving education services, the IDEA's success remains the lodestar.

However, mission creep set in long ago and remains a challenge. The IDEA has continued to expand—in terms of the percentage of students served, numbers of disability categories, and increases in costs, as well as in procedural requirements and complexity. So long as it is an entitlement, we can expect this growth to continue.

We also know that it is compliance driven. The IDEA was set up as a legal compliance and private enforcement due-process system—not an educational-outcome research-based system. Thus, legal process (bureaucrats and lawyers, not educators) drives much of special education. Let's be honest: The IDEA, enacted in 1975, should have had a sunset provision after it achieved its mission of providing access to education for all students with disabilities.[120] Unfortunately, there was no sunset.

Instead, the law and the industry it spawned continued to grow and gradually veered onto the wrong path, as it still follows a twentieth-century input- and rights-driven approach. It has become overly adversarial and procedural, taking educators away from teaching. Teachers spend precious time away from classrooms, doing paperwork, compliance training, and attending meetings. All of the above happen at great expense, even as there is no evidence that the procedures and adversarial climate *improve* student outcomes.

In addition, we know that it is an individual entitlement system that does not equitably teach all students. It singles out one group for special "protections" from schools, impedes the schools' ability to educate all students, and takes educators away from their primary mission: teaching and learning for all. This individual entitlement, without bounds, is not sustainable.

We also know that the private enforcement system is often not fair. It *still* forces parents to protect their and their children's rights by learning the law and becoming their own "attorneys general," even though the law's mission was accomplished. It is no longer needed. A generation or two of children has come and gone since the law's successful achievement. It is time to revisit the premise that parents and students still need 1970s protections.

Based on estimates, we also know that the IDEA costs taxpayers between 21 and 40 percent of school budgets, taking into account both the special- and general-education services it entails. At the very least, so long as special education is a federally funded entitlement statute, Congress needs to require states to report the cost of special education and the cost of educating students with disabilities.[121] Inexplicably, it has never done so.

Finally, and perhaps most damaging, has been the loss of trust between school and home that the current system has created, in spite of the best of intentions. For example, teachers, trained and seeking to provide effective education for their students, are required to practice defensive education, lest a dispute blow up into litigation. Parents who wish to nourish and help their children through the school years need to study the law to fight against the very teachers and schools whose mission is education. It makes no sense. Another example is the two-silo education system the law has created—general and special education. Thus, as discussed above, the current inclusion movement that affects all students, teachers, and parents, has been largely planned and pushed by special-education stakeholders. The voice of general-education teachers and parents, also stakeholders in this enterprise, has been largely missing or muted. To rebuild trust, all voices need to be at the planning table. After all, people are more likely to support what they create, not what is imposed on them.

Undoubtedly, there are many other examples of the damage to trust that the current system has created.

> *Instead of trying to fix the broken system—a fix that has eluded us for decades—let us build on the IDEA's successes and create a twenty-first-century, equitable, and outcome-driven system from the ground up. SPECIAL ED 2.0 proposes to end the individual entitlement for most students with disabilities and their parents, as it is no longer needed to ensure their access to education. All students are in. Ours is an inclusive world. There is no going back. We need to move forward.*

What if we just educate everyone without all the red tape and requirements?[122] What if, without labels, schools focused on the learning, skills, mastery, and knowledge of subjects that students need? While the medical and psychological "labeling" business might dry up, the "education" business will, undoubtedly, pick up.[123]

It is time to begin anew—beyond tweaks of the old. End the twentieth-century model, Special Ed 1.0, and create SPECIAL ED 2.0 for the twenty-first century. The new law keeps what is good, including access to education for all students, targeted individualized education, and the team approach. We need a new law that will provide what the children of the United States need: better outcomes and the pursuit of excellence for all students through proven methods and, generally, more time on task.

The timing for this conversation is fortuitous, as Congress will soon take up the law's reauthorization once again. Congress needs fresh ideas, so it can do more than simply tinker with the old.

Now, a word about change itself. Without a doubt, change is hard. Many folks consider challenging current reality to be taboo—off limits. Too often educators, parents, and others remain silent. Others "vote with their feet" out of public schools.[124] Yet, trying to address broad school reform for all students without seriously examining the truths articulated above is to ignore the needs of twenty-first-century public education in the United States. Let's get real. Current federal law is so twentieth century!

Finally, for those of us who fear change (undoubtedly, most of us do much of the time), in creating SPECIAL ED 2.0, let us be guided by the entrepreneurial Silicon Valley approach: continue to experiment and innovate while building upon the successes that came before. Thus, each new version of technology, such as a smartphone, keeps what's good from the old and moves on to what's better. Dave was right. Just start and get it done!

**Now, on to the new!** [125]

# Part 3: SPECIAL EDUCATION 2.0—Built on five new bedrock directions

| | |
|---|---|
| **Direction 1** | **Equity and excellence for *all* students** |
| **Direction 2** | **New realities and reforms with research-based instruction for students with disabilities** |
| **Direction 3** | **Shared responsibility and clear roles for educators, students, and parents** |
| **Direction 4** | **New school governance structure and collaboration with no individual entitlement** |
| **Direction 5** | **Celebrating the IDEA and reframing our efforts to create SPECIAL ED 2.0** |

Together, these Directions will move all education forward so that it can:

- Be equitable and serve all students with excellence as the goal;
- Serve different groups of students with disabilities per their needs;
- Promote a trust-building partnership among educators, students, and parents, and put education back in the hands of the experts—our nation's educators;
- End the one-group entitlement and create equitable governance structures for all students; and
- Celebrate the success and achievement of Special Ed 1.0, the 1975 law, and bring what works forward.

These new Directions can help bring all parties together for a real conversation to make education right.

## Direction 1: Equity and excellence for *all* students

**A**chieving equity and excellence for all students is extremely challenging. Many educators are already working hard and well to achieve them. Excellent general-education classrooms underlie all effective reform efforts. Without them, we cannot proceed successfully for any student, including students with disabilities.

*"My child has special wants."*

For starters, let's acknowledge that all children are unique and have their own needs and wants. Direction 1 starts where all children start—general education, and focuses on *improving general-education outcomes*, based on the following realities.

First, lawyers don't educate; teachers do! By far, most educators are professional and competent. It is more than time to leave decisions about pedagogy and programs to educators—not to bureaucrats, lawyers, parents, or other outsiders. Teachers need the public's support, instead of the far-too-common criticism, derision, and second-guessing. We need to honor teachers. Precious in-service training time should focus on education in classrooms, not endless paperwork or compliance.[126]

Second, the better general education is, the less special education we need. Effective targeted services and interventions, especially when started early at home for babies and toddlers, reduce the need for special education for many.[127]

Third, all students need orderly instruction in classrooms. Students with or without disabilities cannot routinely or substantially disrupt their own education and the education of their peers. Disturbing data shows that low-income strivers—students from poor families who work hard to achieve—are most affected by classroom disruptions.[128]

Fourth, parents need to step up and do their part to get their children ready for school, because schools can't effectively educate children alone. Hopefully, the Every Student Succeeds Act's (ESSA) focus on family engagement will support this need.

It's time for us to put to work what we know. Adding more requirements and regulations often has the opposite effect; rather than improving classroom practices, they often get in the way of that precious six-hour school day.[129]

Some may scoff at the above and claim that there is a need for laws to protect students with disabilities from incompetent teachers. Perhaps so. But, can't the same be said for general-education students? Sure, there will be some ineffective teachers, some bad apples in the barrel. There may also be educators who are abusive or harassers, or who otherwise act illegally—situations for which we already have laws and procedures. However, it is time to end the IDEA's current preemptive and chilling approaches that involve the micromanagement of classrooms. We need to free educators in their work to improve outcomes for all students—struggling, average, or advanced.

*A THOUGHT OR TWO ABOUT SCHOOL READINESS*

Responding to the fact that many students come to school unprepared for learning, a number of local programs have sprung up around the country starting at the very beginning—with babies and toddlers *at home.* They show great promise and success in helping parents get their children ready to learn. Built on the reality that parents are their child's first teachers, such programs often focus on developing children's early language skills—at home—*before* any preschool.[130]

Yet, the federal buzz these days is about early-childhood programs in schools outside the home. Everyone—from former President Obama to the Every Student Succeeds Act (ESSA)—seems to be on the early-childhood-education bandwagon. Is it the new elixir, the panacea to promote equity and fix our education ills? Congress has poured more than a billion dollars of new money into early-childhood education, focusing on high-needs children.[131] Here is a sample of the exuberance that greeted ESSA's focus on early-childhood programming:

> *[F]or example, the $250 million Preschool Development Grants program will provide invaluable support to states, communities, and programs working to prepare low-income children for Kindergarten and their later development and learning. The program's comprehensive needs assessment and focus on promoting close collaboration within communities, including leveraging existing State Advisory Councils on Early Childhood Education and Care, will ensure existing federal, state, and local resources are used effectively to promote quality and parental choice. Coupled with the program's other core provisions, including encouraging*

*thoughtful strategic planning and promoting sharing of best prac-
tices among early childhood education program providers, will
make a positive difference for the nation's youngest learners and
their families.*[132]

You might wonder, how can one reasonably argue for an approach that
differs from ESSA's new programs? Let's try to do just that.

We agree on the challenge; let's examine the solution. Because
many children come to school unprepared to learn, "we" have to do
something! Right? ESSA's response is to create more early-childhood-
education programs. But let's check out the research before we do that.

The research. The research supports the benefits of a more direct
(and undoubtedly less costly) approach. In the field of education, it makes
sense to pay attention to a child's home situation when he or she comes
to school unprepared. Home is the most practical place to start preparing
children for the social and educational experiences they will have in school.
Home is where children's educations begin with their first teachers—their
parents and caregivers—especially in the vital area of language acquisition. From there, their education can branch out to daycare centers, pre-
schools, or schools.

SPECIAL ED 2.0 suggests that we start in the home because powerful
research supports the efficacy of this approach. In 1995, Professors Betty
Hart and Todd R. Risley turned early-childhood education on its head.[133]
Frustrated by their experience with programs that had no lasting effect on
children's language and growth, they sought a different route. Hart and
Risley tracked verbal interactions in forty-two "well-functioning" families
of infants and their parents in different socioeconomic situations—children
whose parents were middle class/professional, or lower/working class, or

on welfare. Once every month until the children in the study reached age three, the researchers visited their homes, counting the number of words the children experienced.

They discovered that the numbers in the different groups varied widely, creating the now famous "30-million-word gap."[134] That is, children whose parents were on welfare heard and processed a reported 30 million fewer words in the first three years of life than did children of professional parents.

Even if that oft-cited number is too high, the critical point is made: Many children from lower-class or welfare families are not ready for school because of their early life experiences. Some of these children enter the special-education system as students with disabilities, especially children in the categories of students with learning disabilities and speech or language disabilities (which comprise close to 60 percent of all students with disabilities).[135] The bottom line: The importance of early-language acquisition at home cannot be overstated, especially as we know that early gaps continue into the school years.[136]

Given this reality, it is troubling that the latest push for early-childhood education circles back to the earlier, often disappointing institutional programs outside the home. Where is evidence that creating new programs will be effective on a large scale? See the long history of inconclusive evidence for the effectiveness of Head Start, a federally funded program, and similar programs.[137] Of course, there are gems of schools—public and private, regular and charter, but they are not scaled to large systems.

The Economist's "In the Beginning Was the Word" echoes this caution:

> In January (2014), Barack Obama urged Congress and state governments to make high-quality pre-schools available to every

*four-year-old...That is a good thing. Pre-school programmes are known to develop children's numeracy, social skills and (as the term "pre-school" suggests) readiness for school. But they do not deal with the [language] gap in much earlier development that [research has] identified. And it is this gap, more than a year's pre-schooling at the age of four, which seems to determine a child's chances for the rest of his life."[138]*

Why do we not, instead, follow the research on language development and pursue the direct avenue at home? Why do we continue to create programs to try to remediate what children did not learn in the earliest years, instead of proactively working with parents and children in the first place? If parents do not realize how important their role can be, let us take this opportunity—and duty—to share with them the value of talking with, reading to, playing and singing with their babies. The key is to talk, read, and sing!

Pockets of promising efforts are currently under way. A program in Providence, Rhode Island, called "Providence Talks" sends trained visitors into homes to do what is described above. Campaigns for children up to five years old include Too Small to Fail's "Talking is Teaching: Talk, Read, Sing" in various cities; California's "First 5," a state initiative enrolling parents and caregivers in research-supported practices; and "10 Books a Home," which sends volunteers into homes to model literacy and language skills for parents and caregivers. Appendix 2 provides details about sample programs.

In order to ensure equity for young children, we need to scale these in-home efforts toward national policy to help parents be as good at teaching as they can be. They can then send their children to school ready to learn, often without a need for any disability label.

Legal and funding mechanisms for this effort need to be worked out. Will funding come from education, health, and/or human services budgets? How will we assure accountability so that money is well spent in homes? How will collaboration be built between home-based and school-based programs? It's not that we should not pursue better early-childhood out-of-the-home programs; rather, because the data is so powerful, we need to also focus even earlier at home.

Young children need an "all of the above" approach.

## *EXPLORE STANDARDS AND CURRICULA THAT PROMOTE EQUITY AND EXCELLENCE*

Many public schools are doing great work for all students. This new law seeks to set them free to do more of what they already do well. It does not micromanage classrooms; it trusts educators as professionals. Happily, the vast majority don't disappoint. General-education approaches that appear successful and should be explored include these:

- Using challenging and enriched curricula;
- Coaching of new teachers by mentor teachers;
- Implementing early-intervention practices in general-education classrooms when they are research-based and maintain standards;
- Maintaining a "growth mindset" that is built on effort, hard work, and practice;[139]
- Providing valid, reliable, and honest assessments and other
- accountability measures;
- Supporting student-directed and strength-based learning and student grouping; and
- Promoting positive behavioral approaches.

Schools should use only proven practices to improve education opportunities for all.

## USE ADAPTATIONS (ACCOMMODATIONS OR MODIFICATIONS) TO IMPROVE LEARNING, NOT JUST TO GET STUDENTS "THROUGH"

To make education accessible to all students, including students with disabilities, schools often adapt or alter programs, procedures, or standards. Alterations may include adaptations, accommodations, or modifications. Let's define these. Adaptations are changes in programs, procedures, or standards. They include accommodations that *do not fundamentally alter or lower the material, requirements, or standards.* They also include modifications that *do fundamentally alter or lower them.* Adaptations should be provided only when necessary to enhance learning and growth or a student's ability to demonstrate what he or she knows and can do, not merely when they might be helpful or might help the student "pass" or get a better score. Specifically, when providing modifications for a student, the school needs to notify all players—teachers, students, parents, and taxpayers—about how that student's standards were altered. This will keep communication honest and build trust in the system.

On a related issue, let's look at the concept of universal design for learning (UDL), which is now in the Every Student Succeeds Act (ESSA). It grew out of efforts in the 1970s to remove physical barriers for persons with disabilities, and it has since expanded to education in general. It is designed to make all components that support education—including books, equipment, classrooms, and procedures—accessible to the widest feasible range of learners by focusing on how information is presented and how students respond and engage.[140] Certainly worthy goals.

Yet, as worthy as they are, who is watching out for the standards themselves? Who will assure us that UDL does not become a euphemism for dumbing down standards and lowering expectations for all students? This is a critical question, especially as there is much confusion among teachers about what UDL is and isn't. Who monitors when and how reading materials are simplified, work is shortened, "extraneous" graphics are deleted, or language is simplified? Who ensures that standards remain intact? These concerns are worth serious study and conversation.

SPECIAL ED 2.0 urges us to focus on standards without whittling them away. One practical way to build understanding of these issues is to separate the WHAT from the WHO. General educators and state and local policymakers need to decide on and clearly articulate, the WHAT *first*. That is, WHAT are the standards and expectations in general-education classrooms? After that, the WHO—students with disabilities who may need accommodations, modifications, UDL, and the like. To maintain honest standards, it's important for educators to implement the WHAT before the WHO—and to provide transparent information about how students with disabilities (the WHO) are included in those standards. With clarity, educators can create programs that maintain high and clear standards and expectations for all students.

*EXPAND OUR HORIZONS AND "THINK DIFFERENT," AS APPLE DID IN 1997 WITH ITS ADVERTISING CAMPAIGN*

Let's begin by exploring how a sampling of other countries educate students with disabilities.

United States     France     Finland     Philippines     China

In taking a short, impressionistic, and nonscientific "world detour," it becomes immediately clear that, beyond the United States borders, many countries view disabilities or diseases or handicaps—call them what you will—quite differently. In fact, some "disabilities" may actually be cultural constructs.

Since 1975, our worldview has expanded (even as our world seems to have become smaller) for many reasons, including the ease of travel, the Internet, and social media's instant worldwide communication. Our children now compete with children globally. Disability is part of the human condition and is a growing area of civil rights internationally.[141] To begin to explore different approaches to education for students with disabilities in other countries and learn from their views or mindsets, let's take a quick look at France, Finland, the Philippines, and China, sampling large and small countries for some of their perspectives about abilities and disabilities, specifically as they relate to attention-deficit/hyperactivity disorder (ADHD), learning disabilities, and autism.

As one might suspect, the rest of the world does not necessarily share the views of educators and parents in the United States. A positive trait in some cultures may be disabling in others. What works for farmers doesn't work for hunters.[142]

## ADHD in the United States and in France

In the United States, ADHD has grown as a diagnosis and is often treated medically. It's well ensconced in the DSM-5, the latest *Diagnostic and Statistical Manual of Mental Disorders* by the American Psychiatric Association. The DSM-5 is the classification system that drives psychiatric and psychological diagnoses in the United States, and this system in turn seeps into our schools.

The Centers for Disease Control and Prevention (CDC) reported that approximately 11 percent of US children four to seventeen years of age were diagnosed with ADHD in 2011, a percentage that rose from 7.8 percent in 2003.[143] Richard A. Friedman's *New York Times* article "A Natural Fix for ADHD" cites CDC statistics: "6.1 percent of young people were taking some ADHD medication in 2011, a 28 percent increase since 2007."[144]

Why is the diagnosis rising in the United States? Theories abound, including those detailed in Marilyn Wedge's book *A Disease Called Childhood*. Is it, as the author writes, that the industry developing and marketing medications, which the author calls Big Pharma, is joining Big Psychiatry, the industry that seeks new patients (and students) to be "served"? When we realize that ADHD wasn't named until 1987, its rise is even more startling.[145] It is beyond the scope of this little book to further explore the theories and history of the rise of ADHD.

France views and treats ADHD differently. By some reports, France has little ADHD and medicates its children far less than does the United States. A 2012 *Psychology Today* back-and forth-discussion details the dispute about this assertion.[146]

France follows a different classification system, the CFTMEA (Classification Francaise des Troubles Mentaux d L'Enfant et de L'Adolescent).

Largely, the French don't subscribe to the US view that ADHD is biologic, to be treated pharmacologically. Instead, ADHD is viewed as a social and family issue and is generally handled through behavior and adaptive changes and therapies.[147]

## Learning disabilities in the US and in Finland

In the United States, learning disabilities (LD) are called specific learning disabilities (SLD) in the law. In 2013–14, 35 percent of all US students with disabilities were diagnosed with SLD, a disability that is often expected to last a lifetime.[148]

Finland takes a very different view of these disabilities in their various forms. There, children are generally educated without the need for diagnostic labels. Teachers treat students with LD or SLD as having a temporary condition, not a lifetime label, and provide interventions as soon as the students need them. Teachers focus their efforts on teaching students to learn without labeling them first.[149]

## Autism in the United States, the Philippines, and China

In the United States, the number of children diagnosed with autism is rising. In 2014, CNN reported the incidence at one out of sixty-eight children—a rise of 30 percent in only two years.[150] Autism is now called ASD, for Autism Spectrum Disorder, a spectrum disorder that ranges from mild, including Asperger syndrome, to severe and profound. Educating children with autism is a major challenge for US schools. They provide programs with different approaches, including the use of ABA—(Applied Behavioral Analysis), TEACCH (Treatment and Education of Autistic and

Communication Related Handicapped Children), Floortime, SCERTS (Social Communication, Emotional Regulation, and Transactional Support), sensory integration analysis, and others.

About the Philippines—I recently spoke with a businessman who had moved to there with his young-adult son, who has autism. While just anecdotal, I was amazed by his views. When they lived in the United States, his son was in special-education programs. In the Philippines, he was not in school and his medications were stopped. The father reported that they were doing well there and were "much happier." How so?

He explained that his son is viewed differently. For example, when he screams, he is considered to be "happy." Care is given with love around the clock by caregivers. The father said that young people like his son are called "special people," not special *needs* people, and their families are honored for having them. In this father's view, his son functions far better now than he did as a special-education student.

What about autism in China? According to a 2015 *Wall Street Journal* story, "China's Uncounted Children with Autism," China has few services for children with autism and the services that do exist are mostly for children up to age six. Autism Speaks, a US autism-advocacy organization, reported that there were only *four* board-certified Applied Behavioral Analysts (ABA) in the entire country. In comparison, Rhode Island had one hundred one, and California had more than three thousand.

Schools in China are not equipped to educate students with autism. Instead, clinics in China teach parents to work with their children at home. One clinic described in the story "tries to help parents understand and accept their children as they are…[and to show] parents that their children have unique strengths…" [151]

## Emerging shifts in our understanding of disabilities

It's also useful to take a look at emerging shifts in the United States. Some believe that we should get away from the pharmacological-medical approach to disability. Instead of "disabled," some view children as "differently abled." Some question the concept of "ableism" as discrimination against persons with disabilities, and the notion that in order to function as full members of society people with "disabilities" need to be "fixed." For an interesting view of the issues, see Barry Prizant's *Uniquely Human: A Different Way of Seeing Autism.*[152]

Likewise, self-advocacy organizations are springing up. For example, the tagline of Autistic Self-Advocacy Network, a nonprofit run by and for people with autism, is "Nothing about us without us!" Aspies for Freedom, a neurodiversity movement, fights against the medicalization of autism.[153]

Meanwhile, research reveals that some people with autism have strengths in certain fields—hardly handicapping—and links creativity with autism.[154] The current scene is rich with nuance, contradictions, and possibility.

This new law, SPECIAL ED 2.0, proposes that we do a systematic study of representative countries and movements to gather ideas for discussion and, hopefully, promote real change. It's time to "Think Different."

This quick (and surely unscientific) trip around the world enriches our global perspective and provides a window on the variety of views about disability and education. Going forward, how shall we define a disability? What cultural views color our responses? Could special education's foundation that children have a diagnosis for schools to help them overcome (or fix), be mired in twentieth-century thinking? Surely, all important conversation starters.

## TO IMPROVE EQUITY AND EXCELLENCE, REDO HOW WE FUND SPECIAL EDUCATION AND THE EDUCATION OF STUDENTS WITH DISABILITIES

For equity and excellence for all students, the new law proposes an approach to funding that

- places spending caps on educating students with disabilities. At a minimum, open discussion is needed on spending caps and schedules for special-education programming. Continuing this open-ended unsustainable entitlement promotes neither equity nor excellence for all.
- funds only research-based programming. Through objective and valid research and outcome studies, fund only programs *that have a reasonable chance of actually working*. It is time to question sacred cows and break taboos.
- is fully transparent. We, the citizens, have a right to know what is spent to educate students with disabilities—data that Congress has not yet required states to provide. Current data is either unavailable or too complicated, as spending comes from many pockets (often called silos, in education jargon) and becomes virtually unknowable. It is high time for Congress to require states to report expenditures for special education per se as well as the larger amounts to educate students with disabilities (including special- and general-education funding streams). We finally need to ask the key (and heretofore unanswered) question. What is the cost of educating students with disabilities—adding in *both* special and general- education costs—especially in this era when

these students spend most of their time in general-education settings? With full and transparent knowledge, we can begin to create policies that promote equity and excellence for all.

*Let us move to a twenty-first-century model for all children. Objective research, systemic reform, wise and equitable funding, and global examples can be the building blocks for an equitable and excellent system for all.*

## Direction 2: New realities and reforms with research-based instruction for students with disabilities

*SPECIAL ED 2.0 PROPOSES TO DIVIDE STUDENTS WITH DISABILITIES INTO TWO DISTINCT GROUPS*

For the last more than forty years, the IDEA has been a one-size law for all students with disabilities, requiring the same procedures and rights for all. That model no longer serves students well. It has become clear that students with disabilities generally break into two very distinct groups. Let us explore how to better meet student needs.

The relatively small group includes students with severe and profound needs (estimated at 10–20 percent of all students with disabilities or 1–2 percent of all students). These were the students for whom the law was written more than forty years ago, when they were excluded from schools or not served by schools. But twenty-first-century facts differ from those of long ago. *We need a redo!*

Many of these students—including those "with the most severe cognitive impairments"—need intensive, specialized, and comprehensive services. Many of them have education and service needs that are costly in funds and time, creating serious and often unpredictable burdens for school districts, parents, and other agencies. For these and related reasons, it's time to explore the possibility of separating the current service delivery system, governance mechanisms, and funding for this group of students from the majority of students with disabilities.

To do so, the new law, SPECIAL ED 2.0, recommends that a task force be convened and charged with planning a more effective way to educate students with severe and profound needs. Let representative stakeholders, using data and research-based approaches, explore options through an open national conversation. While, of course, the above students are part of the mix of *all* students, the specifics of the new law do not focus on them, pending the results of the task force's recommendations.

The far larger group—80–90 percent of students with disabilities, depending on who is counting—have mild or moderate needs, including specific learning disabilities, speech-language impairments, ADHD, and other disabilities.

Here are a few how-tos to get things started for this far larger group.

## *SPECIAL ED 2.0 BEGINS WITH INTERVENTIONS AND SPECIALIZED INSTRUCTION WITHOUT NEED FOR DIAGNOSTIC LABELS*

Just because we've been labeling students with disabilities since the deaf-education pioneer Abbé de L'Épée began to do so in France in the early 1800s, doesn't mean that we have to continue that practice, particularly as it may not work in twenty-first-century America.[155]

Other countries, as well, struggle with the issue of how to educate students with disabilities. In Ireland, a 2014 report proposed that students with mild disabilities not need *any* diagnosis in order to be provided with services based on current performance and proficiency. The reason given was that the current system was "unfair" and "inequitable," as only wealthy people have access to diagnoses for mild disabilities. To serve all students, the proposal was to have all teachers known simply as "support teachers."[156]

This Irish proposal seems similar to current practices in the Westminster Public Schools in Colorado. A diverse district with more than ten thousand students, it is one of the first in the nation to use a competency-based system. Students move up grade levels, called "performance levels," based on their ability to demonstrate competency in various content areas, such as literacy, math, technology, and personal-social skills. The district's Special Services department's vision statement is "Supporting students' needs ahead of their labels."[157]

This approach is also referred to as the "interventionist framework." It stresses that *all* students does mean *all*—from academically challenged to advanced students. Many teachers are called "interventionists" (not "ELL," "Title I," "gifted and talented," or "special educators"). They assist all students in a timely on-the-spot manner, whether or not they have a diagnostic label for special education. Each student advances at his or her own rate. Dr. Steve Sandoval, the executive director of special services, has stated at various public meetings that the interventionist approach is truly a "multi-tiered system of support on steroids." In 2016, Sandoval was recognized by *Education Week* as one of thirteen "Leaders to Learn From."

Growth mindset. As I see it, this exciting approach substitutes an organic, performance and effort-based process for the more static diagnosis-based process. The growth mindset concept was explored by Stanford University's Carol Dweck in her groundbreaking 2006 book, *Mindset: The New Psychology of Success*. The approach described in this book has exploded on the education scene, with conferences and interest around the world.[158] The growth mindset represents an important shift in thinking about teaching and learning and  aligns well with SPECIAL ED 2.0's approach.

Unlike current law, which views disability categories and labels as static, the growth mindset follows brain research down a different path because, as we are discovering, the brain is malleable and can grow and learn. Dweck distinguishes two types of mindsets—fixed and growth. The fixed mindset assumes that a person has certain intelligence and ability levels that determine his or her achievement and success (for example, the "I'm not good at math" mindset).[159] The growth mindset assumes that a person learns continuously, accepts failure as part of learning, and grows beyond what may have initially been assumed by a label. ("If I work hard, I can learn math!")

Because labels are not neutral, affect students' belief systems, and often create stigma, we should apply them cautiously.[160] Doctors learn, "First, do no harm." So, too, here. This proposed new law seeks to open doors for many students through new approaches, including the growth mindset.

Let's remember that, amazingly, at the time when the old law was established more than forty years ago, parents avoided labeling their children as disabled, not wanting to stigmatize them. Now, they often seek the label, seeing it as the *only* way to receive individualized attention at school. Thus, it is the broken system that drives parent action. SPECIAL ED 2.0 proposes to be child-centric and reduce the need for labels through early targeted interventions and other pedagogical approaches.

Students who need diagnoses. Undoubtedly, some students with disabilities may need a diagnosis to assist educators in individualizing programming for them. In these situations, let educators identify students for special-education services after appropriate interventions and other practices have been tried for a specific time period (perhaps six months) with no measurable growth for the student.

Under the proposals in SPECIAL ED 2.0, for these students, educators can develop student learning plans (SLPs) or other informal documents when services that a student needs clearly differ from those offered in general education, and they can have the authority to revise SLPs efficiently without red tape. In the collaborative approach envisioned by SPECIAL ED 2.0, educators will, of course, provide parents with notice about changes as they occur, consulting with parents as needed. The options for teachers and students will be sufficiently flexible to allow educators to focus on actual on-the-ground student performance and outcomes.

## *LET US MAKE EDUCATION THE GOAL—IN ADDITION TO, NOT INSTEAD OF—MAINSTREAMING/INCLUSION*

In our efforts to educate all students, including students with disabilities, we need to reexamine current mainstreaming/inclusion practices to assure ourselves that they improve results for all students. We need the courage to confront and change what is currently *not* working (or working only with gifted teachers).

Important questions remain: How can we scale efforts beyond pockets of excellence? Does the inclusion focus steer us in the right direction—improved education results for all students? As I see it, the inclusion effort overlooks a better way.

Instead of continuing to focus on placing students with disabilities in the least restrictive environment (LRE), let's look at a promising different approach that places students on the basis of their current needs—not location—the least intervention necessary (LIN). It focuses on educating students according to their current needs, proficiency, and performance—and places them accordingly. *LIN targets services, not placement.* Here is a description of this approach:

> *When professionals attempt to ameliorate problems, standards for good practice call on them to prescribe as much but no more intervention than is necessary. This is essential because interventions can be costly—financially and in terms of potential negative consequences.*

> *The point is: When the focus is on the concept of least intervention needed (rather than LRE) and the concept is approached first*

*from the perspective of need, the primary concern is not about placement, but about a necessary continuum of multifaceted and integrated programs and services for preventing and correcting problems effectively.*

*Moreover, the focus is not just on the individual, but on improving environments so that they do a better job with respect to accounting for individual differences and disabilities. And when the continuum is conceived in terms of integrated subsystems of prevention and early intervention, as well as a subsystem of care, many problems that now require special education can be prevented, thereby ensuring enhanced attention to persons with special needs.*[161]

It is vital to educate students according to their current performance and needs, without overusing aides, aids, accommodations, or modifications that far too often simply mask a student's inability to learn. We should explore LIN as a way forward. If we are truly interested in improving academic and social-skills learning outcomes for all students, let's not make the LRE approach an end in itself. The LRE and LIN concepts need to be flexible so that students with disabilities are well educated as *part* of the mix of *all* students, rather than the main focus of attention. (Sorry for all these acronyms!)

Notably, the Westminster, Colorado Public Schools is implementing the LIN approach. As we move toward "competency-based" schools, the need to discuss the LRE may disappear altogether. High-achieving students can graduate early after reaching competency in all core content areas, while students who struggle, including students with disabilities, can receive mandated services or interventions to accelerate their learning toward *competency*. When grade levels are not the constant, students are taught at their levels. In Westminster, "Learning is the constant. Time is the variable."[162] That says it all, doesn't it?

To get to equitable and effective balances that promote excellence for all students, SPECIAL ED 2.0 proposes that we conduct environmental studies about how LRE and LIN practices affect general-education classmates. These should be conducted from the general-education perspective and considered along with research that we already have from the special-education perspective. Think about it—while we have detailed environmental studies to protect little birds and fishes in fields and streams, we have *none* about how inclusion affects the *learning* environment for all students. Such studies are long overdue.

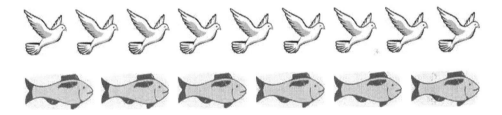

Sometimes, a student's noneducational needs, including issues with medical, mental, or physical health, negatively impact his or her learning or the learning of others and exceed the school's resources and expertise. In such situations, this new law will mandate that other state agencies, including those provide social, medical, child protection, family or judicial services, cost share the services a child needs, along with those that public schools provide.[163] Schools cannot do it alone, lest they be diverted from their primary mission of providing education opportunities for all. Our practices need to be guided by objective research that places learning as a top goal. Only by doing so can we give all students the best chance to be successful and create a just and fair world going forward.

## *LET US BUILD A CLASSROOM CLIMATE TO BENEFIT ALL STUDENTS*

Along with special education came a long history of practices, disputes, and litigation about disruptive classroom behavior. Of course, while many different students—disabled or not—may exhibit such behavior, much litigation has centered on students with disabilities. The issue is often about the relationship of the offending behavior to the student's disability and raises complex public-policy issues that go far beyond the scope of this book.

For now, let's work to build a practical policy for our nation's classrooms. Beyond positive behavioral approaches in general-education classrooms, SPECIAL ED 2.0 prioritizes the need for an orderly, positive learning environment for *all* students, does not contemplate any individual "right" to be in a classroom that trumps the rights of other students to learn. Classroom disruptions appears to affect and slow down all students, as new research appears to demonstrate.[164]  Further, it appears to hurt low-income students who strive to learn the most. "Low-income strivers—impoverished families who follow the rules and work hard to climb the ladder to the middle class—may be the most underserved population in America today" and are the most hurt by students who disrupt classrooms.[165]

In spite of the above, most current reforms, steeped in twentieth-century thinking, persist in heading in the opposite (and I daresay, wrong) direction, focused on one student's rights, not the rights of peers in classrooms—all in the name of fairness and equity. "But when everyone in a school is harmed by some students' unruly behavior, it's a strange notion of fairness indeed."[166]

Schools should no longer be forced to endure extreme disruptive behavior from any student, disabled or not, without recourse. A 2004 *Public Agenda* report, "Teaching Interrupted," found that 85 percent of teachers and 73 percent of parents felt that the "school experience of most students suffers at the expense of a few chronic offenders."[167] Of course, it goes without saying that not all chronic offenders are students with disabilities. However, under current law, students with disabilities have extensive procedural rights that we need to align with their classmates' needs.

In contrast to current practice, SPECIAL ED 2.0 shifts the balance to prioritize and protect the needs that *all* students and teachers have for an orderly classroom environment. As well, we should develop and fund flexible and effective (including alternative) programs for students, disabled or not, who are chronically disruptive.

In short, regarding inclusion and classroom placements for a student who cannot effectively learn in a general-education setting—even if he or she behaves well and gets along with others—that setting is not appropriate. Likewise, if a student's behavior (disability-related or not) chronically interferes with classmates' learning, that class is also inappropriate. We need to be nimble and flexible. The goal is learning for all, not inclusion per se.

In addition, briefly consider these approaches in the proposed new law.

We need to focus on student strengths, not just weaknesses. It appears that others, too, are concerned about special education's long history of a "can't-do" (and learned helplessness) approach and the focus on weaknesses. The Parents Education Network mission statement states that "a strength based approach at school and home is most effective in helping students reach their full potential."[168]

It's time to end the deficit model of education. A major example of turning this view around is our long neglect of vocational- technical-career education, which, happily, appears to be making a comeback.[169]

Compare and contrast these two images of a person in a wheelchair. One is static and passive. The other is more active with a forward-moving seemingly "can do" attitude. This second image was created by the Accessible Icon Project.[170] We need more "can do" in special education!

This inspiring icon leads us again to suggest that we need a new perspective on ability. What *can* a student do? Or, as Dr. Richard A. Villa puts it, "How is the student smart?"[171]

Inspiring also are recent employment trends that promote the hiring of persons with disabilities. For example, a *Wall Street Journal* story, "Companies Find Autism Can Be a Job Skill," reported on efforts in Germany, India, and Ireland to hire persons with autism to fill roles that call for precision, such as debugging software.[172] And a front-page story in Silicon Valley, "Able and Willing—How Silicon Valley Companies are Doing in Hiring People with Disabilities," looks at ways organizations help individuals with disabilities by preparing them for work at various California companies.[173] Since the unemployment rate of adults with disabilities remains far higher than that of adults who are not disabled, let's encourage efforts like these in education as well as business.[174]

> *Of reform efforts, we must ask BIG questions: Are they, research-based, effective, and scalable? Will they improve outcomes for all students, from low-functioning to average to advanced students? Or, do we continue on the ineffective path that raises hopes and hype without supporting data?*

# Direction 3: Shared responsibility and clear roles for educators, students, and parents

### Kids need their sleep

*I visited a wonderful public school in California that seemed to be doing a great job. Excellent program. Fine teachers.*
*Engaged students. Mission-driven for success. In short, the school was operating at full thrust.*

*Yet, the principal told our group of visitors, "If only I could get the parents to put the children to bed early."*

*Schools cannot do it alone. It has to be a joint effort by all.*

We need to keep the roles of educators, students, and parents clear and distinct—in their own spheres.

**The teacher's job** is at school, educating all students in class.

**The parent's job** is at home, providing care and getting children ready for school—for example, assuring that they get enough sleep and that they are as ready as they can be, as discussed in the early-childhood segment above.

**The student's job** is being ready to learn, both at home and at school.

This doesn't mean that there are no overlaps, as parents also have roles and attend meetings, etc., in schools, or that insights shared from parents to teachers, or teachers to parents, will not be of value. But it does mean that, as an overriding generalization, teachers are experts at school, and parents are experts at home.[175]

## *EDUCATORS: SUGGESTED HOW-TOS*

Schools need to support and train educators and other service providers in proven pedagogical approaches that improve student outcomes. They need to strengthen teacher preparation and provide resources for teachers, emphasize curriculum competence and successful approaches to improve outcomes, and de-emphasize compliance training. Educators may need help in becoming active observers so that they can advocate for students at all performance levels in all areas of suspected need, including academic, social, emotional, behavioral, and physical.[176]

Educators (and legislators) should use plain-language principles in documents and at meetings to make information easily accessible to parents and students, as well as teachers, administrators, citizens, and government officials.[177] Minimize acronyms! Get rid of jargon! Provide glossaries and definitions, as needed. Doing otherwise often creates chasms between educators and parents, leading to destructive distrust that helps no one. Instead, we need a common, accessible language for all players in order to rebuild trust. Without that, we create a morass of anger with no winners.[178]

Yet, as described above, several commonly used and misunderstood terms ("doublespeak") create barriers for honest discussion among school personnel and with parents about a child's need, progress, and current performance levels. We need language that is not deliberately euphemistic, ambiguous, obscure—and misleading.

Finally, schools may wish to provide a school-home liaison to ease communication and provide an avenue for sharing concerns without fear. The liaison can be a troubleshooter who helps schools, parents, and students work through issues before they escalate.

Today, we face a teacher shortage across our country, especially in math, science, and special education, with a decline in teacher enrollment in college programs. Some theorize that it is an economic problem, as teaching competes with more lucrative careers. I suspect that it is a combination of economics *and* school climate, a view that was reflected in an *Education Week* report:

> *If an uncertain economy is one likely explanation for the drop, analysts also point to other, less tangible causes: lots of press around changes in teachers' evaluations, more rigorous academic-content*

*standards, and the perception in some quarters that teachers are being blamed for schools' problems.[179]*

There is evidence to support the fact that compliance requirements, assessment mandates, fear of litigation, and related controversies interfere with the joys and satisfaction of teaching, leading some to leave the field. NPR reported that special-education teachers leave the field due to paperwork and compliance pressures.[180] Instead of imposing a tight noose of regulations on them, we need to focus on more time on-task for teachers, lessening their load for other responsibilities. We need to defer to educators as experts and honor them for their hard work and child advocacy. Free teachers to do their magic—*teaching!*

## *STUDENTS: SUGGESTED HOW-TOS*

It is students' responsibility to attend, participate, and learn—to be active in their own education. Education is *not* something that happens *to* students. It is largely what they do for themselves, with support from school and home. When students are unwilling to give it their all, results will inevitably disappoint. This, in turn, affects their classmates as well.

The school's mission is to provide to students an equal opportunity, not assure equal outcomes. The students' mission is to arrive at school ready and motivated to learn. Yet, it is often considered taboo to suggest that student motivation or effort affects or is even relevant to their success, as schools have taken the hit for student failures.[181]

Even so, the media has aired some views on the issue. See, for example, *Newsweek*, "Why School 'Reform' Fails: Student Motivation is the Problem," and the *Atlantic*'s, "The Missing Link in School Reform: Student Motivation."[182] We can hope that the current emphasis on mindset and effort by students may change the perception about students' role in their own learning and progress—an issue for its own book!

Interestingly, some are beginning to question the current special-education system—that, by law, does so much *for* students with disabilities and is reluctant to require effort and hard work *by* them. This approach often leads to overdependence on adults and the above-discussed "learned helplessness," a sense of powerlessness that can grow out of a failure to succeed. Many teachers are beginning to realize that they should do less for students so that students can do more for themselves. For example, the use of 1:1 aides is often questioned. Are they "helping or hovering, as a thoughtful, oft-quoted 1997 piece asked?[183]    Do they create overdependence on adults or other impediments to learning, student effort, and growth?[184] For some students, a clear (and perhaps written) delineation of school and student responsibilities may need to be considered and spelled out among the players.

The law should mandate involvement of other agencies, if needed.

*PARENTS: SUGGESTED HOW-TOS*

Parents are key players in their children's school success. Parental responsibility, engagement, and participation are often vital to a student's achievement at any level. "Decades of research have shown that experiences at home and in neighborhoods have far more influence on children's academic achievement than classroom instruction."[185]

It is encouraging that the Every Student Succeeds Act (ESSA) now focuses on family and parent engagement. Only time will tell what this change accomplishes. In the meantime, it is important to provide parents with guidance, tips, and support to help them contribute to their children's education. And, of course, educators need to demonstrate respect for parents—and vice versa.

For very young children, promising efforts are underway that engage parents and caregivers in the learning process at home—to help narrow readiness gaps for children when they enter kindergarten. These were discussed above. "When parents get the support they need to create a warm, stable, nurturing environment at home, their children's stress levels often go down, while their emotional stability and psychological resilience improve," says Paul Tough, author of *Helping Children Succeed: What Works and Why.*[186]

Educators and other professionals can share with parents the importance of early (*pre*-preschool) language development and help them to speak *with* their children often and naturally. For example, California is undertaking an effort to engage parents in their children's cognitive and language development.[187] *Education Week* recently reported that doctors are the newest group to proselytize for early language development at home, through the American Academy of Pediatrics. "The theory behind the growing number of early-literacy campaigns is that closing the word gap before children start school will help keep them on track to gradu-ate."[188] Appendix 2 lists sample family and home-based efforts around the country, including California First Five, Too Small to Fail, Providence Talks, Ten Books a Home, and others. SPECIAL ED 2.0 advocates for scaling them in order to reach many more families and young children.

As well, it emphasizes parents' responsibility to provide the basics: a reasonable bedtime, a good breakfast and other nutritious meals and snacks, a study routine at home, reading to their children, teaming with teachers, and so forth. "Today, we need the leadership of American mothers, fathers, and all surrogate parents. We need them to begin to develop a standard of excellence in parenting and family, now and for future generations."[189]

And again, the law should mandate other agency involvement, if needed.

Schools and policy makers can provide positive recognition, encour-agement, and incentives for parents. Amanda Ripley's *The Smartest Kids in the World and How They Got That Way* includes an interesting discussion about parenting in other countries. Efforts at home, instead of at school meetings and bake sales, are emphasized. In fact, in many high-performing countries, parents are hardly seen at school.[190] Let's hope that ESSA's new emphasis on family and parent engagement is research-based!

And, of course, to build trust among all players, work together with plain language without doublespeak[191] Doublespeak has no place in SPECIAL ED 2.0. The new law will speak clearly and with transparency. It will also provide honest feedback and information to all players: students, teachers, parents, and citizens. In this way, it will inspire and rebuild trust.

*Respect, honor, and collaboration among educators, students, and parents will go a long way toward improving education outcomes for all students.*

## Direction 4: New school-governance structure and collaboration with no individual entitlement[192]

With the 2015 Every Student Succeeds Act (ESSA), the federal government signaled the way forward. It built flexibility and local control back into education. Amazingly, it does for general education what we need also in special education—it devolves education policy and oversight back to the states and school districts. Senator Lamar Alexander, in announcing ESSA, stated that it is "placing accountability where it belongs—in the hands of states, parents and classroom teachers—[which will] inaugurate a new era of innovation and student achievement in our nation's 100,000 public schools."[193]

For special education, as well, Congress should loosen the federal noose around states and schools and let them evolve, innovate, and build programs flexibly. If Congress refuses to do so, let us ask why students with disabilities and their families and teachers remain singled out for federal control. Would this not be unlawful discrimination?

Direction 4 focuses on building strong and effective home-school relationships *without* the IDEA's individual entitlement. SPECIAL ED 2.0 does not include an individual entitlement for services or due process for most students with disabilities or their parents.[194]

Why not? Arguably, the IDEA's due-process rights might have been appropriate before 1975, when many students with disabilities were excluded from school. Times have changed. Now, all students with disabilities are included in school programming. Our world is far more inclusive than it was more than 40 years ago. Yet, some may fear and argue that without this federal entitlement, these students would again be excluded. So, let us look at several reasons to get us away from programming through fear for the future. First, the reality of our inclusive world is unlikely to change. Second, in this era of pervasive social media, if there were exclusions some place, the world would know it in an instant. Third, general state and federal education and civil rights laws protect all students' rights to public education.   Fourth, given a choice between fear and building on current reality, let us choose the latter and move forward.

Unlike the era that created the IDEA, now all students with disabilities have access to education services. Thus, disputes no longer concern access and rights to an education. Instead, they largely involve educational methods and programming—issues that should be left in the hands of education experts, such as teachers. Lawyers and advocates are ill-equipped to be choosing reading programs for students with specific learning disabilities or pedagogical methods for teaching students on the autism spectrum. Parents (including parents of students with disabilities) are not educational experts, and while their opinions may influence, they should not drive classroom practice through litigation or the threat thereof. In short, the 1975 individual-entitlement, legalistic, and procedural system, designed to ensure access to education, is not well-suited to take us forward in today's world.  Note, parental rights under the IDEA differ markedly from "school choice," vouchers, and charter school options, widely discussed nationally with continuing controversy, especially since the 2016 election of President Donald Trump.[195]

Schools today should focus on research-based services for student outcomes, not inputs and procedures. Sadly, over these forty-plus years, we have gathered *no* evidence that bureaucratic requirements improve student outcomes. Bureaucrats, judges, and lawyers don't teach—teachers do. We need to let them at it. Ending the due-process "private enforcement" system is an overdue and powerful first step.

Of course, there can be no illusion that the entitlement will end any time soon. The huge "mansion" industry made up of evaluators, placement experts, lawyers (of which I am one), state and federal officials, hearing officers and judges, as well as some parents and their advocates, will undoubtedly fight to keep it in place.

Yet, notably, the due-process world is already changing. People are tiring of attending endless IEP team meetings and being bound by rules set up by far-away legislators and bureaucrats instead of by educators. Parents are tired of the paperwork—which often seems like enough to wallpaper their homes! The numbers of hearings and decisions are down nationwide.[196] Causes for this trend may include the fact that most cases settle in a way that is costly for schools (and parents, undoubtedly), with schools "giving away the farm," that hearings are too brutish and painful, and that the results are often disappointing and not proven to be effective. A 2003 US Government Accountability Office (GAO) report about formal disputes in special education notes that federal policymakers have recognized the often adversarial and costly nature of escalated disputes between parents and school districts.[197] In attempting to avoid hearings, many schools settle disputes rather than proceeding with due-process hearings, often forcing school attorneys to be like "claims adjusters."[198] And what, may we ask, does that have to do with education? Add to these realities the fact that the system is neither fair, practical, nor accessible to most parents.[199] In short, it is broken.

Public education is not perfect for any child at all times. In some relatively rare cases (judging by parent-satisfaction surveys), a program for students with disabilities may be ineffective. While that is never good, the same can surely be said for general-education students, many of whom have ineffective programs, drop out of school, or graduate without basic skills. While ineffective programs and outcomes are not limited to students with disabilities, under current law they and their parents have been the only ones entitled to demand and litigate for specified programming. SPECIAL ED 2.0 changes that.

Where is the equity or common sense for us to continue this focus on one segment of our student population? Heretofore, it has been a taboo issue for discussion.

Reformers (even recent state-led task forces) have not ventured into this territory. For example, the 2015 report of California's Special Education Task Force, *One System: Reforming Education to Serve ALL Students* and the 2014 New Jersey report, *Special Education: A Service, Not a Place*, are silent on the entitlement issue.[200]

These reports, among many others, are thoughtful responses to current challenges and mirror several of this proposed new law's Directions, such as early intervention and research-based instruction. They are a good read, filled with important and practical insight and proposals. But—and this is key—they largely keep the current system intact. Through their silence, reports like these envision our system continuing with two distinct silos of students—one with individual legal protection and rights and one (the far larger number) without.

It's all well and good to work for "one system," but is it honest or real when these reports include no discussion of systemic reform of the entitlement provision? This question is especially poignant because general education personnel and parents are often underrepresented at these planning tables. See, for example, above discussions about the California and Washington State special-education task forces whose members were overwhelmingly drawn from the special-education community. To begin to question the underlying taboos that impede systemic reform, we need to hear from all stakeholders.

Meanwhile, back in our nation's classrooms, what's a teacher to do? Obviously, focus time and effort on students who have the right to sue! And we are back to square one—a recipe for continued systemic breakage and erosion of trust and good will. It would be far better public policy to develop a new system for these new times.

*GOVERNANCE: HOW-TOS*

- In the next IDEA reauthorization, push for ESSA's type of flexibility for general-education students also for students with disabilities, their teachers, and parents.
- Give all students and parents access to administrative remedies, state complaint procedures, and state audits that are, of course, available to students with disabilities and their parents. These include dispute resolution at the school and district levels, the right to file complaints with federal and state agencies, and the right to challenge legal rights in courts.
- Focus on facilitating positive relationships between parents, students, and schools in order to resolve disputes through effective, informal, child-centric, and confidential options. End the silos created by the individual entitlement. If appropriate, create new avenues for dispute resolution and trust-building in schools for all students, such as use of an ombudsman or other third-party neutrals.[201] Build bridges and collaboration that focus on positive relationships.

Let's be honest and confront the entitlement directly and honestly. What purpose does it serve now? Who benefits from maintaining it? Is it inertia? "Well, that's the way it's always been, so deal with it."

Is it fear that stops us—the fear that schools will return to the painful era of exclusion, to the era when Eleanor was waved away from the schoolhouse door? In my view, this fear is unwarranted because it is highly unlikely. As discussed above, our society and schools have become more inclusive. And, given today's attitudes and social media, an attempt to again exclude students with disabilities would be stopped in its tracks.

Undoubtedly, such assurances may fall short. Thus, working together to allay these and other fears is key—to be included as part of the proposed national conversation.

Let us seek to be guided by dreams, not fears. Can our nation's time, money, and effort be spent more effectively than by continuing these dysfunctional approaches? Can (or should) we sustain this divided school system? Is there a better way to assure that all students, including students with disabilities, get appropriate learning opportunities?

Yes, there is and yes, we can—starting with that long overdue conversation.

Since such systemic change probably won't happen any time soon, why, you may ask, include a proposal that ends the entitlement? Why open up the possibility of being seen as "anti" children—and especially against the most vulnerable children?

The reality is quite the opposite—the purpose here is to be "pro" all children in our schools. It is time to break taboos and open the conversation so we can dream big to work together to get there for our generation's children, and beyond. Somewhere it has to start. Let it begin here with us.

The Talmudic story about an old man planting a carob tree was retold in 2013 by former President Obama on a trip to Israel, after he planted a tree there.[202] The old man, when asked why he plants trees he'll never see, said, "As my forefathers planted for me, so will I plant for my children." The Greeks said it so: "A society grows great when old men plant trees whose shade they know they shall never sit in." In modern days, the folks who started to march against racial inequality in the 1920s did not live to see the day that Dr. Martin Luther King shared his dream. King did not live to see many of the advances in civil rights that we now take for granted. We, too, may not see these necessary changes, but we can plant the seeds.

Let's not waste more precious resources tinkering with an old broken system. Not addressing the entitlement challenge gets in the way of necessary change.

> *SPECIAL ED 2.0 builds trust, is research—and-outcomes driven, and functions for all students. It ends the entitlement for one small group. Abraham Lincoln warned us, "A house divided against itself cannot stand." So, too, in our schools.*

## Direction 5: Celebrating the IDEA and reframing our efforts to create SPECIAL ED 2.0

We end where we began. Achievements should be celebrated—never taken for granted. The IDEA succeeded. More than 40 years ago, it was revolutionary and ground-breaking. It provides access to school programs and funding for all students with disabilities nationwide. We are grateful for the pioneers—educators, parents, legislators, lawyers, citizens, and other stakeholders—who came before us and fought the good fight— and won.

Toward that end, a group of us in Massachusetts founded Special Education Day in 2005 to do just that—celebrate special education's success and encourage change going forward.[203] We have found that celebrating the current law's successes, allows us to explore better ways forward. We believe we can do better for our students. If you agree, then it's time for that national conversation, to dream big, and ask *what if?*

*Next Steps*

SPECIAL ED 2.0 seeks to move beyond these successes. We need to start the long-overdue national conversation to build a better law so public schools, the backbone of this nation, can be equitable and excellent for everyone. As I see it, continuing to avoid the conversation is risky. Avoidance leaves many voices unheard and encourages, even unwittingly, the further splintering of public education. This splintering leads to the growth of schools for the haves (public, private, elite, home, and others) without addressing the needs of the have-nots (students who can't afford their way out or who nobody wants, in part because they have multiple needs—social, disability, poverty). Also, inadvertently, it may help pave the way for and fuel the current school choice and vouchers push.

Much is at stake for our schools and children. We need to hear from all stakeholders in public education, even those with discordant voices. We need to breaks taboos. As a first step, we need to talk. The time is now.

*"Never doubt that a small group of thoughtful, committed citizens can change the world. Indeed, it's the only thing that ever has."*

—Margaret Mead

It's time to finally talk about that elephant!

Some may balk at *any* discussion that could be perceived to erode any IDEA rights of students with disabilities or their parents. To reiterate, the purpose of SPECIAL ED 2.0 is quite the opposite: It is to refocus our efforts

*"No, this is the elephant."*

back to classrooms (not central offices or courtrooms); to promote learning, not litigation, for all students; to improve outcomes for all students, including students with disabilities; to apply research-based and common-sense practices; to honor educators and support their efforts; to engage parents; and to focus always on providing more time on-task for students and teachers.

To end the two-silo system and get us from here to there, here are a few practicalities.

- Let the 2015 Every Student Succeeds Act (ESSA) be our model. In ESSA, Congress eased federal control over general education and decentralized it to state and school districts. It should begin to consider doing the same for special education and ease the dysfunctional federal controls and entanglements.
- We need to monitor any and all new legislative or administrative proposals (at federal and state levels) to ensure that they explicitly advance the goal of improved outcomes for all students. If they don't, we need to bar such proposals from being imposed on schools, students, and parents.
- We need to confront our fears and free ourselves to build a system that works for all and of which we can be proud. Like a leafy tree, let us work to provide shade and comfort for everyone. Let us begin to talk!

The time is now! Let's work together to build SPECIAL ED 2.0—the start of an effective and excellent *new* law for all students for the twenty-first century. Let's dream BIG, be bold, and, for the sake of children now and tomorrow, explore—*WHAT IF?*

My father has been gone for many years. Yet, he's still inspiring me. I hope that his example encourages us all to dream BIG. Ideas do live on.

**S**PECIAL EDUCATION 2.0—Breaking Taboos to Build a NEW Education Law breaks out of the special-education reform mold. Instead of merely recommending fixes and tweaks for the current system—that have been tried without success—it dares to propose an innovative, second generation law for all students, general and special education. Specifically, it proposes five Directions that create a dynamic blueprint for a new inclusive and optimistic law for all students. It invites us to open an honest national conversation without the taboos that have thwarted innovation and discussion.

A bit of history. SPECIAL ED 2.0 celebrates the nation's forty-plus-year-old special-education law because it succeeded in providing access to education for all students with disabilities. We now educate more than six million students (13–14 percent of US students) under this law—a strong foundation to build upon.

Yet, despite that success, the old 1975 law—let's call it Special Education 1.0—became dysfunctional in many ways. It is too focused on compliance and paperwork, not outcomes; its onerous procedural requirements impede schools, educators, parents, and students; its "wait to fail" approach often provides services too late; and its adversarial system pits parents against educators, creating warring stakeholders—yes, even inside our public schools!

A better way. SPECIAL ED 2.0 starts with a laser focus on improving general-education outcomes for *all* students (from the neediest strugglers to the most advanced). Why? We know that better general education means we will need less special education. Here are its five Directions.

**Direction 1**—Focuses on equity and excellence for *all* students with challenging standards and timely interventions, through objective research-based approaches. For example, it balances mainstreaming/inclusion with the education needs of all students. SPECIAL ED 2.0 frees teachers to teach and parents to parent. It funds programs equitably for all students.

**Direction 2**— Boldly reflects *modern* needs and realities of students with disabilities. The world has changed radically since 1975—and so have the students served by special education. No longer centered on those with significant and profound needs (just 10–20 percent of today's cohort), 80–90 percent of students served by special ed have mild and moderate needs.

**Direction 3**— Defines and requires positive participation by educators, students, and parents. Each has a vital role to play in this partnership.

**Direction 4**— Creates a trust-building, collaborative governance structure and approach for all groups of students, without an individual entitlement for any group.

**Direction 5**— Builds on the current foundation to create a successful *new* law for all students.

You are invited to join in, think BIG, and dream aloud. Together, let us ask—*WHAT IF?*

# Appendix 1
## Glossary of acronyms and basic terms

**Accommodation**—A change in course, test, location, timing, student response or other attributes which is necessary to provide access for a student with a disability to participate and demonstrate academic achievement and functional performance that does not fundamentally alter or lower the standards or expectations. An accommodation is sometimes called an "appropriate accommodation."

**Adaptation**—The umbrella term for a change in the IEP or Section 504 plan for a student with a disability that may include accommodations, modifications, aids, benefits, and services. The term "adaptation" does not involve the concept of the effect of changes on standards or expectations.

**ADHD**—Acronym for "attention-deficit/hyperactivity disorder."

**"All" students**—Describes 55 million students in US public schools, including general- and special-education students, English-language learners, average, "at risk," advanced, gifted—all means all!

**ASD**—Acronym for "autism spectrum disorder."

**CDC**—Centers for Disease Control and Prevention, part of the federal Department of Health and Human Services.

**Competency-based education**—Systems of instruction, testing, grading, and academic reporting that are based on students demonstrating that they have learned the knowledge and skills that they are expected to learn as they progress through their education, according to The Glossary of Education Reform website (edglossary.org).

**DSM**—*The Diagnostic and Statistical Manual of Mental Disorders* is the classification and diagnostic tool of the American Psychiatric Association. The latest version is the DSM-5, published in 2013.

**DOE**—US Department of Education.

**Differentiated instruction**—A method for teaching students with different ability levels and ways of learning in the same classroom through different lessons and methods designed to meet individual needs.

**ESSA**—Every Student Succeeds Act (2015), latest iteration of the ESEA (Elementary and Secondary Education Act) and successor to the NCLB (No Child Left Behind Act).

**FAPE**— Acronym for "free appropriate public education."

**GAO**—The federal Government Accountability Office.

**General education**—Includes regular classrooms and other supports all students may receive, such as math labs, small group literacy instruction, and before and after school tutoring. Sometimes called GE, general ed, or gen ed.

**G & T**—Gifted and talented students.

**Growth mindset**—An educational perspective that focuses on children's learning through hard work and perseverance, from *The New Psychology of Success* by Carol S. Dweck, PhD.

**IDEA**—Individuals with Disabilities Education Act, a federal law enacted in 1975 to guide education activities in the United States; last reauthorized in 2004.

**IEP**—Acronym for "Individualized Education Program," required by current law for students with disabilities.

**Inclusion**—A term that pertains to the Congressional preference for students with disabilities to participate in general-education classrooms. Also called mainstreaming. In the United States, it generally means educating general- and special-education students in the same classrooms with the same curriculum. UNESCO uses it to mean that all children including girls, poor students, and others are educated.[204]

**Intervention**—Providing appropriate educational supports and services to students early so they don't fall behind.

**LIN**—Acronym for "least intervention necessary," a concept that focuses on services and differs from LRE, which focuses on placement.

**LRE**—Acronym for "least restrictive environment." Often this refers to a general-education classroom that, under current law, places a student with a disability in a class with nondisabled peers to the "maximum extent appropriate."

**Modification**—A change in course, test, location, timing, student response, or other attributes which is necessary to provide access for a student with a disability to participate and demonstrate academic achievement and functional performance and which fundamentally alters or lowers the standards or expectations. Also called "nonstandard accommodation."

**MTSS**—Acronym for "multi-tiered system of supports."

**NCES**—National Center for Education Statistics.

**NCLB**—Not Child Left Behind Act,

**OSEP**—Office of Special Education Programs in the US Department of Education.

**OSERS**—Office of Special Education and Rehabilitative Services in the US Department of Education.

**Plain language**— www.plainlanguage.gov. The federal website defines it as: Plain language (also called Plain English) is communication your audience can understand the first time they read or hear it. Language that is plain to one set of readers may not be plain to others…No one technique defines plain language. Rather, plain language is defined by results—it is easy to read, understand, and use.

**RDA**—Acronym for "results-driven accountability."

**Special education**—Identification, evaluation, and individualized service provision for students with disabilities mandated by the federal Individuals with Disabilities Education Act (IDEA) and state laws; sometimes referred to as SE or special ed.

**RTI**—Acronym for "response to intervention, response to instruction."

**SLD**—Acronym for "specific learning disabilities." Students with SLD account for approximately 35 percent of all students with disabilities.

**SLP**—Acronym for "student learning plan."

**Student(s) with disability(ies)**, per current law—The makeup of these students nationally has changed since 1975. Students with disabilities with profound or severe needs, such as intellectual impairments, deafness, blindness, and severe autism, for whom the law was originally enacted, account for 10–20 percent of students with disabilities served today. Some 80–90 percent of students with disabilities have mild or moderate needs, including specific learning disability (SLD), speech-language impairments, ADHD (attention-deficit/hyperactivity disorder), and others.

# Appendix 2
## A sampling of promising efforts in home-based early-childhood education

**A**n Ounce of Prevention. Since 1982, the Ounce of Prevention Fund has pursued a single goal: that all American children—particularly those born into poverty—have quality early childhood experiences in the crucial first five years of life. Its mission statement says, "The Ounce of Prevention Fund gives children in poverty the best chance for success in school and in life by advocating for and providing the highest-quality care and education from birth to age five." http://www.theounce.org

**First 5 California.** Created in 1998 by taxpayers, this advocacy organization funds programs that "invest in integrated programs and resources designed to benefit three target audiences: the Child, the Teacher, and the Parent..." According to its website, "Research shows 90 percent of a child's brain develops in the first five years of life. Making those years count is what *First 5 California* is all about. Our focus is to educate parents and caregivers about the important role they play in their children's first years." http://www.first5california.com

**Providence Talks.** Its website states, "Providence Talks proposes to do something never before attempted at the municipal level: to intervene at a critically early age, from birth to age four, to close the 30 million word gap at a city-wide scale and ensure that every child in Providence enters a kindergarten classroom ready to achieve at extraordinary levels." Providence Talks has been featured in *The New Yorker* ("The Talking Cure"), *The New York Times* ("The Power of Talking to your Baby"), and other publications. http://www.providencetalks.org

**10 Books A Home.** Its website states, "Ten Books A Home is a nonprofit organization that offers a new early education solution to families in High Poverty Communities..." http://www.10booksahome.org

**Too Small to Fail**. Talking, reading, and singing at home is teaching! This organization's goal is to help parents, caregivers, businesses, and community work together using brain-based research to help children ages zero to five in the areas of brain development, learning, and health to increase their chances for success as they get older. http://www.toosmall.org

**Zero to Three.** This independent, nonpartisan, research-based organization was created in 1977. Its mission is to "advance the proven power of nurturing relationships by transforming the science of early childhood into helpful resources, practical tools, and responsive policies for millions of parents, professionals and policymakers." http://www.zerotothree.org

# Appendix 3
## Promising efforts that bring people together

**Living Room Conversations.** This organization's website states that it is a "new, open-source project exploring the power of revitalized civil discourse in America." www.livingroomconversations.org

**Coalition for Public Safety.** "Unlikely Cause Unites the Left and the Right: Justice Reform," *The New York Times*, February 19, 2015, page 1. It's wonderful that we have a model—how the right and left have come together to fix our justice system through a new organization, the Coalition for Public Safety. It brings together a most unlikely combination of leaders from right and left, including Koch Industries, Center for American Progress, many from both sides of the aisle in Congress, and President Obama. http://www.coalitionforpublicsafety.org/

**NO Labels.** This organization focuses its efforts on trying to achieve cooperation between political parties and the administration. "Stop fighting! Start fixing!" states the website. https://www.nolabels.org/

**All Sides.** The goal of this crowd-driven news organization is to balance views and biases from all sides. According to the organization's website,

"All Sides sees a strong connection between our ability to comprehend and tolerate different opinions, and our ability to develop better schools, more jobs, more well-being, and less violence. So we decided to address the core problem—the overwhelming and often one-sided information flow." http://www.allsides.com/

# Acknowledgments

So many people helped me along the way and I'm most grateful. Dave Burgess encouraged me to "just do it!" at our café that Sunday morning; my Special Education Day Committee colleagues, Carla B. Jentz, Marilyn "Bonnie" Bisbicos, and Ed Orenstein shared years of spirited discussion and planning; Martina Jecker coached me to go for it; Charlotte Koskoff shared her political savvy and education insight, and Susan Wolfe, her expertise in book preparation; John Merrow provided super helpful feedback; Steve Sandoval inspired me by building programs that in many ways are models for this proposed new law; and Nikki Zapol continues to enrich me with insightful edits, friendship, and wisdom.

The list of friends and colleagues who indulged me with fruitful (sometimes, heated) discussions, debate, and insights is long and rich—Carolyn Bell, Mary Bevernick, Matthew Brown, Maureen Burness, Steve Case, David Choi, Jack Clarke, Monica Conrad, Ben Davidowitz, Anne Delfosse, Ann Marie Dubuque, Richard Epstein, Mary Grady, Douglas Green, Rick Hanushek, Thomas Hehir, Philip Howard, Jim Keith, Vera Kenehan, Michael Kirst, Bill Koski, Nate Levenson, Doreen Lohnes, Diana McDonough, Colleen Messing, Georgiana Miranda, Gordana Pavlovic, Teri Perl, Mike Petrilli, Sasha Pudelski, Gary Ruesch, my Stoneman Chandler & Miller LLP friends and colleagues, Steven Stone, Cheryl Theis, Jim Thomeczek, Sonja

Trainor, Jim Walsh, Ron Wenkart, Esther Wojicki, and Jerry Zelin. And editors: Susan Ferguson, Jessica Swift and Tom Parker.

Finally, of course, my wonderful family—Dan, Julie, Paul, and Sora—and my personal friends—many of whom encouraged me through endless talk and frets in getting this book from start to happy finish.

The opinions and errors are mine.

# About the Author

**M**iriam Kurtzig Freedman, JD, MA, is a lawyer and education thought leader. Her writings have appeared in *Education Week*, *The Wall Street Journal, Education Next, Hoover Digest, The University of Chicago Law Review Online, Diane Ravitch's Blog*, and *The Atlantic.com*. She has written six books in law and education.

As a lawyer, Miriam represented Massachusetts public schools for many years. Before that, she was a hearing officer and a teacher in California, New Jersey, New York, and Massachusetts.

As a reformer, Miriam wrote *Fixing Special Education: 12 Steps to Transform a Broken System* (2009), which spurred reforms. In 2005, she co-founded Special Education Day, a national holiday, to honor special education's success and spur reform, including SpedEx, the Massachusetts Alternate Dispute Resolution Model.

Miriam received her law degree from New York University, a Master of Arts from the State University of New York at Stony Brook, and a Bachelor of Arts from Barnard College (Columbia University).

When not engaged in the above, Miriam enjoys long daily walks, spending time with friends and family (especially her granddaughter!), and, of course, hanging out at the café.

For more information, please visit Miriam's website, www.schoollawpro.com.

# Suggested resources

California Statewide Special Education Task Force. *One System: Reforming Education to Serve All Students.* http://www.smcoe.org/assets/files/about-smcoe/superintendents-office/statewide-special-education-task-force/Task%20 Force%20Report%205.18.15.pdf

Dweck, Carol. *Mindset: The New Psychology of Success.* New York: Ballantine Books, 2006.

Finn, Chester E., Jr., Andrew J. Rotherham, and Charles R. Hokanson Jr., eds. *Rethinking Special Education for a New Century.* Washington, DC: Thomas B. Fordham Foundation and the Progressive Policy Institute, 2001.

Finn, Chester E., Jr., and Brandon L. Wright. *Failing Our Brightest Kids: The Global Challenge of Educating High-Ability Students,* Cambridge: Harvard Education Press, 2015.

Ford, Richard Thompson. *Rights Gone Wrong: How Law Corrupts the Struggle for Equality.* New York: Farrar, Straus and Giroux, 2011.

Freedman, Miriam Kurtzig. *Fixing Special Education: 12 Steps to Transform a Broken System*. Austin TX and Boston MA: Park Place Publications and School Law Pro, 2009.

Freedman, Miriam Kurtzig. "Special Education: Its Ethical Dilemmas, Entitlement Status, and Suggested Reforms." *University of Chicago Law Review Online*. Volume 79, Issue 1, May 7, 2012.

Freedman, Miriam Kurtzig. "Mainstreaming Special Ed Students Needs Debate," *Wall Street Journal*, August 4, 2013.

Gartner, Alan and Dorothy Kerzner Lipsky. "Beyond Special Education: Toward a Quality System for All Students." *Harvard Education Review*, 57:4, December 1987, 367-96.

Gladwell, Malcolm. *The Tipping Point: How Little Things Can Make a Big Difference*. Boston: Little, Brown and Company, 2000.

Glendon, Mary Ann. *Rights Talk: The Impoverishment of Political Discourse*. New York: The Free Press, 1991.

Hehir, Thomas. *New Directions in Special Education: Eliminating Ableism in Policy and Practice*. Cambridge, MA: Harvard Education Press, 2005, 2010.

Howard, Philip K. *Life without Lawyers: Restoring Responsibility in America*. New York: W.W. Norton & Co., 2009.

Howard, Philip K. *Rule of Nobody: Saving America from Dead Laws and Broken Government*. New York: W.W. Norton & Co., 2015.

Meredith, Bruce and Julie Underwood. "Irreconcilable Differences? Defining the Rising Conflict Between Regular and Special Education." *Journal of Law and Education*, 24:2, 1995.

Pasachoff, Eloise. "Special Education, Poverty, and the Limits of Private Enforcement." *Notre Dame Law Review* 86, no. 4, 2011.

President's Commission on Excellence in Special Education. *A New Era: Revitalizing Special Education for Children and their Families*. Washington DC: US Department of Education, 2002. https://education.ucf.edu/mirc/Research/President's%20 Commission%20on%20Excellence%20in%20Special%20Education.pdf.

Prizant, Barry. *Uniquely Human: A Different Way of Seeing Autism*. New York: Simon and Schuster, 2015.

Pudelski, Sasha. *Rethinking Special Education Due Process*, American Association of School Administrators. April 2013.

Ripley, Amanda. *The Smartest Kids in the World: How They Got That Way*. New York: Simon and Schuster, 2014.

Sahlberg, Pasi. *Finnish Lessons: What Can the World Learn from Educational Change in Finland?* New York: Teachers College Press, 2011.

Sinek, Simon. *Start with Why.* New York: Penguin Books, 2009.

Sternberg, Robert and Elena Grigorenko. *Our Labeled Children: What Every Parent and Teacher Needs to Know about Learning Disabilities.* New York: Perseus, 1999.

Teicholz, Nina. *The Big Fat Surprise: Why Butter, Meat and Cheese Belong in a Healthy Diet.* New York: Simon & Schuster, 2014.

Wedge, Marilyn. *A Disease called Childhood: Why ADHD Became an American Epidemic.* New York: Penguin Group, 2015.

# Endnotes

1.  Much has been made of the fact that the 1963 speech by Martin Luther King, Jr., was "I Have a Dream," not "I have a plan." Dreams can powerfully move us forward. Simon Sinek quotes, http://www.azquotes.com/quote/714927

2.  Stories are real; names have been changed to protect privacy.

3.  In 1975, the law was called the EAHCA (or EHA), the Education for All Handicapped Children Act, 20 USC 1400 et seq. In 1990, it was renamed as the Individuals with Disabilities Education Act (IDEA). Here, the term IDEA is used for all versions.

4.  Philip K. Howard, *Rule of Nobody: Saving America from Dead Laws and Broken Government* (New York: W.W. Norton & Co., 2015), p. 126.

5.  *Board of Education v. Rowley*, 458 US 176 (1982). While this book was written, the Supreme Court heard the *Endrew F. v Douglas County School Board* case that involves the level of benefit that the law requires schools to provide to students with disabilities. A decision is pending.

6.  Bruce Meredith and Julie Underwood, "Irreconcilable Differences? Defining the Rising Conflict Between Regular and Special Education," *Journal of Law and Education*, 24:2 (1995).

7.  In particular, see *P.A.R.C. v. Commonwealth of Pennsylvania,* 334 F. Supp. 1257 (E.D. PA 1971) and *Mills v. Board of Education,* 348 F. Supp. 866 (D.D.C. 1972).

8. Sasha Pudelski, *Rethinking Special Education Due Process*, American Association of School Administrators, April 2013, p. 5, http://www.aasa. org/uploadedFiles/Policy_and_Advocacy/Public_Policy_Resources/Special_ Education/AASARethinkingSpecialEdDueProcess.pdf

9. The IDEA was amended or reauthorized in 1983, 1986, 1990, 1997, and 2004. Email exchange with Professor Mitchell Yell, July 20, 2016.

10. Mary Ann Glendon, *Rights Talk: The Impoverishment of Political Discourse,* (New York, Free Press, 1991), Page X in Preface. A personal word. I read this book, perhaps 20 years ago. It explained how the creation of new individual rights silences a focus on and conversation about the common good. Perhaps this book resonated with me because I experienced my early childhood in countries that focus more on community and the common good than on individual rights.

11. See note 4. Howard, *Rule of Nobody*, quoting a school principal, p.126.

12. See *Lau v Nichols*, 414 US 563 (1974), regarding non-English-speaking school children. Neither English language learners nor their parents have an individual entitlement to services or due process. See also Miriam Kurtzig Freedman, *Meeting NCLB's Mandate: Your Quick-Reference Guide to Assessments and Accountability* (LRP 2nd ed, 2008).

13. Eloise Pasachoff, "Special Education, Poverty, and the Limits of Private Enforcement," *Notre Dame Law Review* 86:4 (2011), pp. 1413, 1421 n 23.

14. This realization is not new. From early days, its challenges were clear. See, for example, "Paperwork is Number 1 Obstacle for Special Education Teachers," *CEC Today*, April/May 1998, p.14, http://files.eric.ed.gov/fulltext/ED420141.pdf; and Lisa Gubernick and Michelle Conlin, "The Special Education Scandal," *Forbes*, February 10, 1997, http://www.forbes.com/forbes/1997/0210/5903066a.html

15. Anthony Lewis, review of Philip K. Howard's *Life without Lawyers: Restoring Responsibility in America* (New York:W.W. Norton & Co. 2009), in the *New York Review of Books*, April 9, 2009.

16. See, for example, Miriam Kurtzig Freedman, *Fixing Special Education: 12 Steps to Transform a Broken System* (Austin TX and Boston MA: Park Place Publications and School Law Pro, 2009); and Freedman, "Special Education: Its Ethical Dilemmas, Entitlement Status, and Suggested Reforms," *University of Chicago Law Review Online,* https://lawreview.uchicago.edu/sites/lawreview.uchicago.edu/files/uploads/79_1/Freedman.pdf

17. 20 USC 1411(a) (2).

18. "Federal stimulus package increases special education funding," *Pacesetter* 32:2 (Summer 2009) p. 1, http://www.pacer.org/newsletters/pacesetter/summer09.pdf; and "Individuals with Disabilities Education Act Funding Distribution," *Atlas: New America* (2015), http://atlas.newamerica.org/individuals-disabilities-education-act-funding-distribution

19. Janie Scull and Amber M. Winkler, "Shifting Trends in Special Education," *Fordham Institute* (2011), http://edexcellence.net/publications/shifting-trends-in-special.html

20. See, for example, Stephen Lipscomb, *Resolving Special Education Disputes in California*, Pacific Policy Institute (February 2009).

21. National Center for Education Statistics (NCES), http://nces.ed.gov/programs/coe/indicator_cgg.asp

22. Denis P. Doyle, "Letter from Washington: All Children Can Learn," *Association for Supervision and Curriculum Development,* that includes a discussion of the mixed meaning of the term, http://www.ascd.org/publications/educational-leadership/oct03/vol61/num02/All-Children-Can-Learn.aspx

23. See Special Education Day at www.specialeducationday.com; also "The IDEA 40th Anniversary," US Department of Education (DOE), http://www2. ed.gov/about/offices/list/osers/idea40/index.html; and "CEC Celebrates 40 Years of IDEA," Council for Exceptional Children, http://www.cec.sped.org/ Policy-and-Advocacy/IDEA-40

24. Michelle R. Davis, "President Ford's Legacy Includes a Special Education Law He Signed Despite Worries," *Education Week*, January 3, 2007, http://www. edweek.org/ew/articles/2007/01/03/18ford_web.h26.html

25. As enacted, S. 6, approved November 29, 1975, is Public Law 94-142 (89 Stat. 773).

26. 20 USC 1414(d) (1) (B).

27. 34 CFR Part 300.8. For European medical classification model, see Sarah L. Triano, "Categorical Eligibility for Special Education: The Enshrinement of the Medical Model in Disability Policy," *Disability Studies Quarterly* 20:4 (Fall 2000), http://dsq-sds.org/article/view/263/275

28. The law and regulations still use the term "mental retardation." 20 USC 1401 (3); 34 CFR 300.8 (c) (6). Other terms in current use include "cognitive impairment" or "intellectual disability."

29. *OSEPs Annual Reports to Congress on the Implementation of the (IDEA)* from 1995-2015 features the breakdown of student characteristics, http:// www2.ed.gov/about/reports/annual/osep/index.html. The NCLB testing and accountability guidelines created an alternate assessment option for 1–2 percent of the total number of students tested who have "the most significant cognitive impairments." When this book was written, ESSA testing policies were unsettled.

30. Chester E. Finn Jr., Andrew J. Rotherham, and Charles R. Hokanson Jr., eds., summary of chapter 2, "Time to Make Special Education 'Special' Again," by Wade F. Horn and Douglas Tynan, in *Rethinking Special Education for a New Century* (Washington, DC: Thomas B. Fordham Foundation and

the Progressive Policy Institute, 2001), www.ppionline.org/ndol/print.
cfm?contentid=3344

31. President's Commission on Excellence in Special Education, *A New Era: Re-vitalizing Special Education for Children and their Families,* (Washington DC: US Department of Education, 2002), https://education.ucf.edu/mirc/Research/ President's%20Commission%20on%20Excellence%20in%20Special%20Education.pdf; see also Freedman, *Fixing Special Education*, pp. 7-8; Erin Dillon of Education Sector concluded that four categories—SLD, S/L impairment, OHI, and ED—account for more than 70 percent of all students with disabilities; Robert Sternberg and Elena Grigorenko, *Our Labeled Children: What Every Parent and Teacher Needs to Know about Learning Disabilities* (New York: Perseus, 1999), p. 12.

32. *Understanding Subgroups in Common State Assessments: Special Education Students and ELLs,* NCEO Brief, National Center on Educational Outcomes (July 2011), http://www.cehd.umn.edu/NCEO/onlinepubs/ briefs/brief04/brief04.html. See also *The Condition of Education 2016,* Institute of Education Sciences, and National Center for Education Statistics, US Department of Education, http://nces.ed.gov/programs/ coe/pdf/coe_cgg.pdf

33. *The State of Learning Disabilities,* Third Edition, 2014, National Center for Learning Disabilities, p.12, https://www.ncld.org/wp-content/ uploads/2014/11/2014-State-of-LD.pdf. *The Condition of Education 2016,* Institute of Education Sciences, National Center for Education Statistics (NCES) in the DOE, http://nces.ed.gov/programs/coe/pdf/coe_cgg. pdf; and "Fast Facts: Students with Disabilities," Institute of Education Sciences, NCES, https://nces.ed.gov/fastfacts/display.asp?id=64

34. Diagnoses may be based on the discrepancy model or a history of interventions—a discussion that is not fleshed out in this book.

35. G. Reid Lyon, Jack M. Fletcher, Sally E. Shaywitz, Bennett A. Shaywitz, Joseph K. Torgesen, Frank B. Wood, Ann Schulte, and Richard Olson, "Rethinking Learning Disabilities," in Finn et al., *Rethinking Special Education,* pp. 259, 268–269, 282, https://edexcellence.net/publications/rethinkingsped.html

36. Dr. Douglas Green, "Why Does Special Education Have to Be Special?" *Education Week,* July 5, 2015; and Kevin P. Dwyer, "Rights without Labels: Words or Actions?" *Communique,* the Newspaper of the National Association of School Psychologists, 35:3 (2006), p. 36.

37. Joe Humphreys, *The Irish Times,* June 19, 2014, http://www.irishtimes.com/news/education/you-are-hoping-for-a-worse-diagnosis-when-the-child-is-going-to-school-it-s-terrible-1.1837307

38. Generally, 20 USC 1414.

39. See note 16. Adapted from Freedman, *Fixing Special Education,* p. 9.

40. Lee Hale, "It's Not Easy Teaching Special Ed," NPR, January 2, 2016, http://www.npr.org/sections/ed/2016/01/02/461590749/its-not-easy-teaching-special-ed

41. See note 13. Pasachoff, "Special Education" and Professor Bill Koski, Stanford University School of Law, personal conversations and emails.

42. Tice Palmaffy, "Evolution of the Federal Role," in Finn et al., *Rethinking Special Education,* p. 15. Palmaffy cites *Back to School on Civil Rights,* issued by the National Council on    Disability (2000).

43. For example, most parents appear to be satisfied with IEP process. See Wade E. Fish, "The IEP Meeting: Perceptions of Parents of Students Who Receive Special Education Services," *Preventing School Failure: Alternative Education for Children and Youth,* 53:1 (2008), http://www.tandfonline.com/doi/abs/10.3200/PSFL.53.1.8-14; and Santa Monica, Calif., parent survey results, http://www.smmusd.org/press/press1415/SpecialEdSurveyResults.pdf

44. Perry Zirkel, *Education Law Reporter*, vol. 302, as reported by *Education Week (May 15, 2014)*; see also, this data: In 2010-2011, California had 678,000 students with disabilities. Parents (or schools, in a small number of cases) filed for 2,495 hearings or mediations and the state issued decisions in 105 cases. Massachusetts numbers are similar: In 2011, of 166,000 students with disabilities, parents rejected 8,348 IEPs (one-half of 1 percent of all IEPs). Of these, there were 544 hearing and 809 mediation requests (a small percentage of these were by schools). The state issued 35 decisions that year. See Christina Samuels, "A Few States Spawn Most Complaints on Special Education, Study Says," *Education Week*, May 15, 2014, http://blogs.edweek. org/edweek/speced/2014/05/a_few_states_spawn_most_compla.html

45. Miriam Kurtzig Freedman, "Special education in California needs more flexibility," *EdSource*, July 16, 2012, http://edsource.org/2012/special-education-in-california-needs-more-flexibility/17444

46. Nanette Asimov, "Extra-special education at public expense," *San Francisco Chronicle*, February 19, 2006.

47. Kim Goodrich Ratcliffe testimony before Health, Labor, and Pension Committee, US Senate, "IDEA: What's Good for Kids? What's Good for Schools?" March 21, 2002.

48. See "Special Education—State and Local-Imposed Requirements Complicate Federal Efforts to Reduce Administrative Burdens," *US Government Accountability Office*, January 8, 2016, p. 10, http://www.gao.gov/products/GAO-16-25

49. See note 47. Ratcliffe testimony, "Reform needs to occur when a law is so vaguely written that litigation is required to give it definition. The IDEA is such a statute. Due process is a brutal system. It paralyzes the educational system; it paralyzes individuals," http://ftp.resource.org/gpo.gov/hearings/107s/78448.pdf

50. See note 19. Scull and Winkler, "Shifting Trends in Special Education," pp. 12, 15.

51. See discussion above. Inadequate funding has dogged this law for many years. Sam Allis, "The Struggle to Pay for Special Ed," *TIME*, November 4, 1996, pp. 82-83; Lisa Gubernick and Michelle Conlin, "The Special Education Scandal," *Forbes*, February 10, 1997, pp. 68-70; and more recently, Alison Leigh Cowan, "Amid Affluence, A Struggle over Special Education," *New York Times*, April 24, 2005.

52. For a thoughtful discussion, see the 2013 California Legislative Analyst Report, "Overview of Special Education in California," *Legislative Analyst's Office*, http://www.lao.ca.gov/reports/2013/edu/special-ed-primer/special-ed-primer-010313.aspx#6

53. J.S. Kakalik, W.S. Furry, M.A. Thomas, M.F. Carney, "The Cost of Special Education: Summary of Study Findings," prepared by the Rand Corp. for the DOE, November 1981, http://www.rand.org/content/dam/rand/pubs/reports/2006/R2858.pdf. See also Stephen Lipscomb, Students with Disabilities and California's Special Education Programs, *Public Policy Institute of California*, January 2009, http://www.ppic.org/content/pubs/report/R_109SLR.pdf

54. https://nces.ed.gov/fastfacts/display.asp?id=66

55. 34 CFR 300.116 (e); *Letter to Wohle*, 50 IDELR 138 (OSEP 2008).

56. See note 19. Scull and Winkler, "Shifting Trends in Special Education," p. 12, cited in Nathan Levenson, *Boosting the Quality and Efficiency of Special Education*, Fordham Institute (2012).

57. See note 53, Lipscomb's 2009 *PPIC* report, p. 4.

58. According to the Special Education Expenditure Project report, "What Are We Spending on Special Education Services in the United States, 1999-2000?" special-education costs were $50 billion ($8080 per special-education student) with $27.3 billion additional general-education services for students with

disabilities—totaling $77.3 billion ($12,474 per special-education student). The cost for general-education students at the time was $6556 per pupil. The Report, updated June 2004, by Jay G. Chambers, SEEP Director Thomas B. Parrish, CSEF Director Jenifer J. Harr. Submitted to DOE, Office of Special Education Programs, http://csef.air.org/publications/seep/national/advrpt1.pdf

59. See Alessandra Perna, "Breaking-the-Cycle-of-Burdensome-and-Inefficient-Special-Education-Costs-Facing-Local-School-Districts," *New England Law Review*, 49, Spring 2015, p. 541.

60. Jan and Bob Davidson with Laura Vanderkamp, *Genius Denied: How to Stop Wasting Our Brightest Young Minds* (New York: Simon & Schuster, 2004).

61. "Jacob K. Javits Gifted and Talented Students Education Program," DOE, http://www2.ed.gov/programs/javits/index.html

62. http://blogs.edweek.org/edweek/speced/2014/01/gifted_education_special_educa.html

63. The 6 percent figure, informal discussion, March 15, 2016 with the executive director of the National Association for Gifted Children. Also see "Frequently Asked Questions about Gifted Education," *National Association for Gifted Children*, http://www.nagc.org/resources-publications/resources/frequently-asked-questions-about-gifted-education; and Chester E. Finn Jr. and Brandon L. Wright, "The Bright Students Left Behind," *Wall Street Journal*, August 19, 2015, http://www.wsj.com/articles/the-bright-students-left-behind-1440024541

64. Jill Barshay, "Top US students fare poorly in international PISA test scores, Shanghai tops the world, Finland slips," *Education by the Numbers*, December 2, 2013, http://educationbythenumbers.org/content/top-us-students-fare-poorly-international-pisa-test-scores-shanghai-tops-world-finland-slips_693/

65. Mark Kelman, "Moral Foundations of Special Education Law," in Finn, et al, *Rethinking Special Education*, pp. 78, 82, 84. See also note 15. Howard, *Life*

*without Lawyers,* and see note 31. Sternberg and Grigorenko, *Our Labeled Children.*

66. See note 42. Palmaffy, "Evolution of the Federal Role," in Finn, et al, *Rethinking Special Education,* p. 8.

67. *36th Annual Report to Congress on the Implementation of the Individuals with Disabilities Education Act, 2014,* DOE, http://www2.ed.gov/about/reports/annual/osep/2014/parts-b-c/36th-idea-arc.pdf

68. Collecting federal data about English-language learners is growing. See "English Language Learners in Public Schools," *Institute of Education Sciences, National Center for Education Statistics,* May 2016, http://nces.ed.gov/programs/coe/indicator_cgf.asp

69. http://www.impatientoptimists.org/Posts/2014/03/We-care-about-what-we-measure-and-measure-what-we-care-about-Gates-Foundation-and-Grand-Challenges-Canada-partner-on-Saving-Brains#.WBD4Pi0rLz1

70. "Frequently Asked Questions," *National Association for Gifted Children,* http://www.nagc.org/resources-publications/resources/frequently-asked-questions-about-gifted-education

71. See Ingfei Chen, "By Not Challenging Gifted Kids, What Are We Losing?" *Mindshift/KQED News,* April 25, 2014, http://ww2.kqed.org/mindshift/2014/04/25/what-do-we-risk-losing-by-not-challenging-gifted-kids/; and see note 62. Barshay, "Top US students;" Deirdre V. Lovecky, "Exploring Social and Emotional Aspects of Giftedness in Children," *Supporting Emotional Needs of the Gifted,* http://sengifted.org/archives/articles/exploring-social-and-emotional-aspects-of-giftedness-in-children; and "Social and Emotional Issues," *National Association for Gifted Children,* http://www.nagc.org/resources-publications/resources-parents/social-emotional-issues

72. See Melanie Natasha Henry, Comment, *No Child Left Behind? Education Malpractice Litigation for the 21st Century,* 92 Cal L Rev 1117, 1166 (2004),

noting "[t]here is no explicit private right of action for parents and students within the NCLB." See also *Assn of Community Orgs for Reform Now v New York City Dept of Educ*, 269 F. Supp. 2d 338, 344 (S.D.N.Y. 2003), holding "it is clear that Congress did not intend to create individually enforceable rights with respect to the notice, transfer or ....services provisions contained in the NCLB."

73. Every Student Succeeds Act (ESSA). President Barack Obama's signing statement,    December 10, 2015.

74. Bruce Mohl and Jack Sullivan, "Isn't Every Child Special?" *CommonWealth*, March 2009, 34-47, at UNZ.org website, https://www.unz.org/Pub/CommonWealth-2009q1-00034

75. Work by T. K. Gilhool (1989) cited in Jeremy Ford, "Educating Students with Learning Disabilities in Inclusive Classrooms," *Electronic Journal for Inclusive Education*, 3:1, Fall/Winter 2013, p. 3, http://corescholar.libraries.wright.edu/cgi/viewcontent.cgi?article=1154&context=ejie

76. Adayinourshoes.com

77. Letter to Wohle, 50 IDELR 138 (OSEP 2008); 20 USC 1412 (a) (5).

78. See note 5 discussion of *Endrew F.Douglas County*, a case pending at the Supreme Court.

79. When general-education students are discussed, arguments for inclusion include these. First, when students with disabilities are included, students *without* disabilities benefit from the understanding and compassion they develop. Second, students experience the "democracy means here comes everybody" world. Third, the LRE gives general-education kids a chance to teach and model that fosters increased self-confidence. Fourth, the belief (whither data?) that the general-education students' education is not harmed. For example, see "Concerns About and Arguments Against Inclusion and/or Full Inclusion," http://www.sedl.org/change/issues/issues43/concerns.html; and see Kids Together that promotes inclusive

communities, http://www.kidstogether.org/inclusion/benefitsofinclusion. htm. While these arguments may have validity, their source—inclusion advocates—raises concern. Where are objective studies from the general ed perspective—environmental studies on how inclusion affects    all students?

See also Miriam Kurtzig Freedman, "Mainstreaming Special Ed Students Needs Debate," *Wall Street Journal*, August 4, 2013, http://online.wsj.com/news/articles/SB10001424127887323309404578613532497541300

80. See Robert Osgood, "Chapter 3: Challenging Traditions in Special Education," *The History of Inclusion in the United States* (Washington DC: Gallaudet University Press), http://gupress.gallaudet.edu/excerpts/HIUS.html; and Jeremy Ford, "Educating Students with Learning Disabilities in Inclusive Classrooms," http://corescholar.libraries.wright.edu/cgi/viewcontent.cgi?article=1154&context=ejie

81. 347 US 483 (1954). www.principalspartnership.com/inclusionlre.pdf (website under construction).

82. Tom Parrish, "Special Education Expenditures, Revenues, and Provision in California," *American Institutes for Research as a Partner in the California Comprehensive Center at WestEd*, December 2012, v, http://www.smcoe.org/assets/files/about-smcoe/SpEd%20Expenditures,%20Revenues,%20Provision%20in%20CA.pdf

83. See, for example "Review of Special Education in the Commonwealth of Massachusetts: A Synthesis Report" (August 2014), commissioned by the Massachusetts Department of Elementary and Secondary Education, http://www.doe.mass.edu/sped/hehir/2014-09synthesis.pdf; WrightsLaw, http://www.wrightslaw.com/info/lre.incls.rsrch.whitbread.htm; Maryland Coalition for Inclusive Education, http://www.mcie.org/usermedia/application/6/inclusion_works_final.pdf; and the Special Education Guide at http://www.specialeducationguide.com/pre-k-12/tools-and-research/scholarly-and-evidence-based-research-ar-

ticles/, https://www.wested.org/project/california-inclusion-and-behavior-consultation-network/ among many other sources.

84. Carmen Constantinescu and Christina A. Samuels, "Inclusive Classes have Downsides, Researchers Find, *Education Week*, Vol. 36, NO. 3, September 7, 2016. Research reported by Michael A. Gottfried and his colleagues at the University of California, Santa Barbara, and follows earlier research by Jason Fletcher at the University of Wisconsin-Madison. He coined the term, "the spillover effect."

85. See note 84 above.

86. Frederick M. Hess, "The Responsibility of Edu-scholars in the Public Square," *Education Week*, January 11, 2016, http://www.edweek.org/ew/articles/2016/01/13/the-responsibility-of-edu-scholars-in-the-public.html

87. Nick English, "Everyone was Wrong: Saturated Fat Can Be Good for You," *Greatest*, November 21, 2013, http://greatist.com/health/saturated-fat-healthy; and Jo Willey, "Eating fat is good for you: Doctors change their minds after 40 years," *Express*, October 23, 2013, http://www.express.co.uk/life-style/health/438600/Eating-fat-is-good-for-you-Doctors-change-their-minds-after-40-years

88. "Part B State Performance Plan and Annual Performance Report Part B Indicator Measurement Table," *IDEA State Performance Plan/Annual Performance Report (SPP/APR)*, DOE, https://www2.ed.gov/policy/speced/guid/idea/bapr/2014/2014-part-b-measurement-table.pdf

89. Mike Baker, "Turning Point for Special Needs?" *BBC News*, June 10, 2005.

90. Thomas Hehir, *New Directions in Special Education: Eliminating Ableism in Policy and Practice* (Cambridge, MA: Harvard Education Press, 2005, 2010), pp. 68, 69.

91. The California Statewide Special Education Task Force had 33 members. Approximately 24 or 25 represented special education—special educators,

administrators, professors, parents of students with disabilities, and persons otherwise involved with special education. This left, at most, eight or nine members (fewer than 30 percent) representing general education. Because some members wore several hats, such as being both special-education directors and general-school administrators at various times, it is hard to be precise. "Statewide Special Education Task Force Report," *San Mateo County Office of Education,* March 2015, http://www.smcoe.org/about-smcoe/state-wide-special-education-task-force/

The Washington Statewide Special Education Task Force included 228 participants, representing 138 organizations. About 35 percent may have represented general education, while the rest came from special education. "On the Creation of a Statewide Special Education Task Force," *Washington State Governor's Office of the Education Ombuds,* November 2014, http://oeo.wa.gov/wp-content/uploads/SpecialEdTaskForce-Report_Nov2014.pdf

Since both states identify about 10 percent of their students for special education and most students with disabilities spend most of their time in general-education classrooms, future task forces should consider having the percentage of participants at the planning meetings representing the general-education community closer to 90 percent!

92. Phone conversation, April 7, 2016.
93. See "Dear Colleagues" letters by OSEP and OSERS, promoting MTSS for students with dyslexia, and FAPE in inclusive education. Michael K. Yudin letter, October 23, 2015, https://www2.ed.gov/policy/speced/guid/idea/memosdcltrs/guidance-on-dyslexia-10-2015.pdf and Michael K. Yudin and Melody Musgrove letter, November 16, 2015, https://www2.ed.gov/policy/speced/guid/idea/memosdcltrs/guidance-on-fape-11-17-2015.pdf
94. See Chester R. Finn Jr., "Is differentiated instruction a hollow promise?" *Thomas B. Fordham Institute,* May 1, 2014, http://www.k12accountability.org/resources/

Gifted-Education/Is_Differentiated_Instruct_Hollow.pdf. For controversy, see *Education Week's* Commentary by James R. Delisle, "Differentiation Doesn't Work," in which he called it a "failure, a farce, and the ultimate educational joke played on countless educators and students." That piece "provoked an avalanche of reader comments. Because of the extraordinary level of interest in the essay, *Education Week* published a response by one of differentiated instruction's foremost proponents, Carol Ann Tomlinson," http://www.edweek.org/ew/articles/2015/01/07/differentiation-doesnt-work.html?qs=delisle, January 7, 2015; http://www.edweek.org/ew/articles/2015/01/28/differentiation-does-in-fact-work.html?qs=delisle, January 28, 2015.

95. See note 94 above.

96. Tom Loveless, "The Resurgence of Ability Grouping and the Persistence of Tracking," *Brookings*, March 18, 2013, http://www.brookings.edu/research/reports/2013/03/18-tracking-ability-grouping-loveless; and Petrilli, "All together now;" and Courtney A. Collins and Li Gan, "Does Sorting Students Improve Scores," *National Bureau of Economic Research*, February 2013, http://www.nber.org/papers/w18848

97. See note 6. Bruce Meredith and Julie Underwood, "Irreconcilable Differences?" p. 217.

98. Lake Wobegon is a fictional town created by Garrison Keillor on the Prairie Home Companion radio show.

99. Whether we should expect all students to graduate at the same rate and time raises public-policy issues that we leave for another day.

100. http://nces.ed.gov/programs/coe/indicator_coi.asp; http://eddataexpress.ed.gov/data-element-explorer.cfm/tab/trend/deid/4542/state/US/http://nces.ed.gov/ppubs2008/2008031.pdf

101. http://www.npr.org/sections/ed/2016/04/27/475628214/most-high-school-seniors-arent-college-or-career-ready-says-nations-report-card

102. Anya Kamenetz et al., NPR, June 5, 2015, http://apps.npr.org/grad-rates/

103. Editorial Board, "The Counterfeit High School Diploma," *New York Times*, December 31, 2015, p. A20.

104. Robert J. Samuelson quoting Kirst, "School 'Reform' and Student Motivation," *Newsweek*, September 6, 2010.

105. Arne Duncan, "Equity and Education Reform: Secretary Arne Duncan's Remarks at the Annual Meeting of the National Association for the Advancement of Colored People (NAACP)," DOE, July 14, 2010, http://www.ed.gov/news/speeches/equity-and-education-reform-secretary-arne-duncans-remarks-annual-meeting-national-association-advancement-colored-people-naacp

106. Michael J. Petrilli, *Thomas B. Fordham Institute*, February 23, 2016, https://edexcellence.net/articles/stop-with-the-political-correctness-and-just-admit-it-lots-of-high-school-graduates-arent

107. Honestygap.org; http://all4ed.org/articles/proficient-versus-prepared-new-achieve-report-highlights-honesty-gaps-in-more-than-half-of-states-student-proficiency-ratings/

108. John D'Auria, Presentation at Special Education Day, Waltham, Massachusetts, December 4, 2014, http://www.teachers21.org/

109. See note 16. Freedman, *Fixing Special Education*, p. 73.

110. David Ginsburg, "Unlearning Learned Helplessness," *Education Week Teacher*, March 8, 2014, http://blogs.edweek.org/teachers/coach_gs_teaching_tips/2014/03/unlearning_learned_helplessness.html

111. Carol Dweck, *Mindset: The New Psychology of Success* (New York: Ballantine Books, 2006).

112. See note 16. Freedman, *Fixing Special Education*, p. 16; and *A New Era*, pp. 11-12, 17.

113. *Webster's Ninth Collegiate Dictionary* (1988).

114. See note 40. Hale, "It's Not Easy Teaching Special Ed," NPR, *January 2, 2016.*

115. See note 114 above.

116. "Overview of Results-Driven Accountability: Assuring Compliance and Improving Results," *Massachusetts Department of Elementary and Secondary Education,* August 2014, http://www.doe.mass.edu/sped/osep/ AssuringCompliance-RDA.pdf

117. 2011 CADRE (National Center on Dispute Resolution in Special Education) 5th National Symposium on Dispute Resolution in Special Education, Eugene, Oregon.

118. GAO, "Special Education—State and Local-Imposed Requirements Complicate Federal Efforts to Reduce Administrative Burdens."

119. "The Hidden Half: School Employees Who Don't Teach," *Thomas B. Fordham Institute,* August 12, 2014. http://edexcellence.net/publications/ the-hidden-half

120. Philip K. Howard, "The Crippling Hold of Old Law," *Wall Street Journal,* April 2-3, 2016, p. C3.

121. Federal funds only partially cover special-education costs, forcing states and districts to pay the balance, often taking funds from other programs. "The impact of special education on education reform: A case study of Massachusetts," in Finn, et al, *Rethinking Special Education*; also see a California study, "How is Special Education Funded in California," Legislative Analyst's Office, http://www.lao.ca.gov/reports/2013/edu/ special-ed-primer/special-ed-primer-010313.aspx#6

122. See discussion above about students who may need more intensive services and who are included in the discussion of *all* students, though their rights and legal structure may be different.

123. See note 16. Freedman, *Fixing Special Education*, pp. 56-57.

124. See note 79. Those parents, who can, pull their children out of public schools and place them in private school or choose to home-school them. Freedman, "Mainstreaming Special Ed Students Needs Debate."

125. Road sign in Australia. I thank my colleague Geoffrey Bok for sharing this image.

126. See note 47. Ratcliffe, "IDEA: What's Good for Kids."

127. "Why Early Childhood Investments Work," *The Ounce*, http://www.ounceofprevention.org/about/why-early-childhood-investments-work; Joanne Jacobs, "Beyond the Factory Model," *Education Next,* 14: 4 (Fall 2014), http://educationnext.org/beyond-factory-model/; "The Importance of Early Intervention for Infants and Toddlers with Disabilities and their Families," *The National Early Childhood Technical Assistance Center* (2011), http://www.nectac.org/~pdfs/pubs/importanceofearlyintervention.pdf; James W. Stigler and James Hiebert, *The Teaching Gap: Best Ideas from the World's Teachers about Improving Education in the Classroom* (New York: The Free Press, Simon and Schuster, 1999, 2009); Pasi Sahlberg, *Finnish Lessons: What Can the World Learn from Educational Change in Finland?* (New York: Teachers College Press, 2011); *A New Era*. See Appendix 2 for organizations involved in home-based early childhood education.

128. Michael Petrilli, "Disruptive Students Hurt High Achievers Most," *Bloomberg View,* November 3, 2015, http://www.bloombergview.com/articles/2015-11-03/disruptive-students-hurt-high-achievers-most

129. Jamie Vollmer, "The Ever Increasing Burden on America's Public Schools," http://www.jamievollmer.com/poster.html

130. Paul Tough, "To Help Kids Thrive, Coach Their Parents," *New York Times,* May 21, 2016, http://www.nytimes.com/2016/05/22/opinion/sunday/to-help-kids-thrive-coach-their-parents.html?_r=1; Nicholas Kristof, "Building

Children's Brains/Too Small to Fail," *New York Times,* June 2, 2016, http://www.nytimes.com/2016/06/02/opinion/building-childrens-brains.html

131. Joe Heim, "Early childhood education gets push from $1 billion federal investment," *Washington Post,* August 1, 2016, https://www.washingtonpost.com/local/education/early-childhood-education-gets-push-from-1-billion-federal-investment/2016/07/31/a288d948-55bb-11e6-b7de-dfe509430c39_story.html

132. Charles Joughin, "See How Early Childhood Came Out a Big Winner in ESSA," *First Five Years Fund,* December 11, 2015, http://ffyf.org/see-how-early-childhood-education-came-out-a-big-winner-in-essa/

133. Betty Hart and Todd R. Risley, *Meaningful Differences in the Everyday Experiences of Young American Children* (Baltimore: Paul H. Brookes Publishing, 1995).

134. The study was more nuanced, detailing the types of conversations, positive and negative, and parental directives that children heard, but this summary suffices here. "The Thirty Million Word Gap," *School Literacy and Culture, Rice University,* http://literacy.rice.edu/thirty-million-word-gap

135. "Fast Facts: Students with Disabilities," *National Center for Education Statistics,* https://nces.ed.gov/fastfacts/display.asp?id=64. More than 20 years after that Hart and Risley research, these findings are still relevant and powerful, with follow-up studies at Stanford University, the University of Chicago, and elsewhere.

136. Jessica Lahey, "Poor Kids and the Word Gap," *The Atlantic,* October 16, 2014, http://www.theatlantic.com/education/archive/2014/10/american-kids-are-starving-for-words/381552/; Mai Miksic, "The Persistent Achievement Gaps in American Education," *CUNY Institute for Education Policy,* March 20, 2014, http://ciep.hunter.cuny.edu/the-persistent-achievement-gaps-in-american-education/; and Julia B. Isaacs, "Starting

School at a Disadvantage: The School Readiness of Poor Children," *Brookings Institution,* http://www.brookings.edu/~/media/research/files/papers/2012/3/19%20school%20disadvantage%20isaacs/0319_school_disadvantage_isaacs.pdfzebra

137. See, for example, disappointing history of Head Start's lasting effect on preparing young children for school. https://www.washingtonpost.com/news/answer-sheet/wp/2013/03/05/does-head-start-work-for-kids-the-bottom-line/; http://www.usnews.com/news/articles/2015/08/03/report-scant-scientific-evidence-for-head-start-programs-effectiveness; see also Christina Samuels, "Study Casts Fresh Doubts on Durability of Pre-K Gains," Education Week, October 7, 2015.

138. Feb. 22, 2014, http://www.economist.com/news/science-and-technology/21596923-how-babbling-babies-can-boost-their-brains-beginning-was-word

139. See note 111. Dweck, *Mindset* offers an excellent discussion of the difference between a growth and fixed mindset. I believe it's the best book for educators and parents. Chris Hildrew, "Becoming a growth mindset school," *Teaching: Leading Learning,* March 21, 2014, http://chrishildrew.wordpress.com/2014/03/21/becoming-a-growth-mindset-school/; Holly Yettick, "Studies Offer Practical Ways to Bring 'Growth Mindset' to Schools," *Education Week,* April 6, 2014, http://blogs.edweek.org/edweek/inside-school-research/2014/04/studies_provides_practical_ins.html. But see Alfie Kohn's, "The Downside of 'Grit," April 6, 2014, http://www.alfiekohn.org/miscellaneous/grit.htm

140. "What is UDL?" *National Center on Universal Design for Learning,* http://www.udlcenter.org/aboutudl/whatisudl; "About Universal Design for Learning," *CAST,* http://www.cast.org/our-work/about-udl.html#.

VrfB6_krLqA; and "Universal Design for Learning (UDL): Applying Universal Design Concepts to Postsecondary Learning," University of Hawaii, http://www.ist.hawaii.edu/downloads/presentations/pdf/ApplyingUniversalDesignConcepts.pdf

141. Edurne Garcia Iriate, Roy MConkey, and Robbie Gilligan (Eds.), *Disability and Human Rights: Global Perspectives* (Basingstoke, UK: Palgrave Macmillan, 2015); and *World Report on Disability*, World Health Organization (2011), http://www.who.int/disabilities/world_report/2011/chapter1.pdf

142. See "Thom Hartmann's Hunter and Farmer Approach to ADD/ADHD," *Thom Hartmann Program*, November 1, 2007, http://www.thomhartmann.com/articles/2007/11/thom-hartmanns-hunter-and-farmer-approach-addadhd

143. "New Data: Medication and Psychological Services Among Children Ages 2-5 Years (Healthcare Claims Data)," *Centers for Disease Control and Prevention*, http://www.cdc.gov/ncbddd/adhd/data.html

144. Richard A. Friedman, "A Natural Fix for A.D.H.D.," *New York Times*, Oct. 31, 2014, http://www.nytimes.com/2014/11/02/opinion/sunday/a-natural-fix-for-adhd.html

145. Marilyn Wedge, *A Disease called Childhood: Why ADHD Became an American Epidemic* (New York: Penguin Group, 2015); and see that ADHD used to have other names, including "minimal brain dysfunction," "hyperkinetic reaction of childhood," and "ADD (attention deficit disorder) with or without hyperactivity." https://en.wikipedia.org/wiki/Attention_deficit_hyperactivity_disorder

146. See note above. Wedge, "Why French Kids Don't Have ADHD," *Psychology Today*, March 8, 2012, https://www.psychologytoday.com/blog/suffer-the-children/201203/why-french-kids-dont-have-adhd; and Stephanie Sarkis, PhD, "French Kids Do Have ADHD: An Interview," *Psychology Today*, Sept. 22, 2012,

https://www.psychologytoday.com/blog/here-there-and-everywhere/201209/french-kids-do-have-adhd-interview

147. See note above and recent articles exploring these issues. Bronwen Hruska, "Raising the Ritalin Generation," *New York Times*, August 18, 2012, http://www.nytimes.com/2012/08/19/opinion/sunday/raising-the-ritalin-generation.html?_r=0; and see note 145. Wedge, "Why French Kids," *Psychology Today.*

148. "Children and Youth with Disabilities" (chart), *The Condition of Education 2016*, NCES, p. 96, http://nces.ed.gov/pubsearch/pubsinfo.asp?pubid=2016144

149. See note 127. Sahlberg, *Finnish Lessons;* and Amanda Ripley, *The Smartest Kids in the World: How They Got That Way* (New York: Simon and Schuster, 2014).

150. Miriam Falco, "Autism Rates Now 1 in 68 in US Children" CDC," *CNN*, March 28, 2014, http://www.cnn.com/2014/03/27/health/cdc-autism/

151. Shirley S. Wang, "China's Uncounted Children with Autism," *Wall Street Journal*, May 18, 2015, http://www.wsj.com/articles/chinas-uncounted-children-with-autism-1431963548. Of course, there are many different views of autism around the world.

152. Thomas Hehir, *New Directions in Special Education; Readings for Diversity and Social Justice*, Third Edition (New York: Routledge, 2013); Barry M. Prizant, PhD, *Uniquely Human: A Different Way of Seeing Autism*, (New York: Simon & Schuster, 2015).

153. See Autistic Self-Advocacy Network, http://autisticadvocacy.org/home/about-asan/; and Aspies for Freedom, http://www.aspiesforfreedom.com/

154. Ariana Eunjung Cha, "Study: Autism, creativity and divergent thinking may go hand in hand," *Washington Post*, August 25, 2015, https://

www.washingtonpost.com/news/to-your-health/wp/2015/08/25/
study-autism-creativity-and-divergent-thinking-may-go-hand-in-hand/

155. See note 27. Triano, "Categorical Eligibility," *Disability Studies Quarterly.*

156. Joe Humphreys, "Schools support system to be reformed," *The Irish Times,* June 19, 2014, http://www.irishtimes.com/news/education/schools-support-system-to-be-reformed-1.1837260. I don't know if these reforms were implemented.

157. http://www.westminsterpublicschools.org//site/default.aspx?PageID=168

158. For example, "Growth Mindsets in Practice Conference 2016," *OSIRIS Educational,* http://osiriseducational.co.uk/mindsets-conference.html; and "Shaping Student Mindsets," *Learning and the Brain,* http://www.learningandthebrain.com/Event-328/Shaping-Student-Mindsets/Program

159. See also Matthew B. Crawford, "The Case for Working with Your Hands," *New York Times,* May 21, 2009, www.nytimes.com/2009/05/24/magazine/24labor-t.html; and Julie Lythcott-Haims, Review of *The Gift of Failure* by Jessica Lahey, *New York Times,* August 18, 2015, http://www.nytimes.com/2015/08/23/books/review/the-gift-of-failure-by-jessica-lahey.html and http://www.jessicalahey.com/the-gift-of-failure/

160. Much is written about the stigmatizing effect of labels; for example, C.P. Gibson, "Overcoming the stigma of the learning disability label: A story of survival and recovery." *ACA Special Education News,* Article LD-8-3, http://www.acadcom.com/acanews1/anmviewer.asp?a=53; and Dara Shifrer, "Stigma of a Label—Educational Expectations for High School Students Labeled with Learning Disabilities," *Journal of Health and Social Behavior,* 54:4, December 2013, pp. 462-480, http://hsb.sagepub.com/content/54/4/462.abstract

161. "Least Intervention Needed: Toward Appropriate Inclusion of Students with Special Need," *UCLA Center for Mental Health in Schools, Department of Psychology* (2015), http://smhp.psych.ucla.edu/pdfdocs/leastint/leastint.pdf

162. "Our Competency Based System," *Westminster Public Schools,* http://www.cbsadams50.org/

163. This is a complex issue. "Interagency agreements" with other state agencies have often been ineffective, in part because they are based on funding in those agencies. That is, other agencies provide services only if they have funds—in stark contrast to public schools that are mandated to provide services, no matter what their budgets include. We need explicit mandates for other agencies to step up.

164. See note 84.

165. See note 128. Petrilli, "Disruptive Students," *Bloomberg View.*

166. See above note.

167. http://www.publicagenda.org/files/teaching_interrupted.pdf

168. http://www.parentseducationnetwork.org/About-Us/Our-Mission/

169. See, for example, http://www.usnews.com/news/business/articles/2016-04-27/career-education-making-a-comeback-in-us-high-schools; http://www.educationworld.com/a_news/career-education-making-comeback-529673905

170. The Accessible Icon Project, http://accessibleicon.org/. I thank David Manzo, President/Executive Director of the Cotting School in Lexington, MA, for sharing this image with me.

171. Dr. Richard A. Villa, *Bayridge Consortium,* http://www.ravillabayridge.com/

172. March 28, 2014.

173. Sue Dremann, "Able and Willing," *Palo Alto Weekly Online,* September 25, 2015, http://www.paloaltoonline.com/print/story/2015/09/25/able-and-willing

174. US Department of Labor, Office of Disability Employment Policy (ODEP); https://www.dol.gov/odep/

175. Based on discussion with Diana McDonough, retired education attorney, Fagen Friedman & Fulfrost LLP.

176. Time on task research. See Samuel E. Abrams, "The Mismeasure of Teaching Time," *Center for Benefit-Cost Studies of Education,* Teachers College, Columbia University, January 2015, http://cbcse.org/wordpress/wp-content/uploads/2015/01/The-MismeasureofTeachingTime-SA-1.14.15.pdf; and Sarah D. Sparks, "Do US Teachers Really Teach More Hours?" *Education Week,* February 2, 2015, http://www.edweek.org/ew/articles/2015/02/04/do-us-teachers-really-teach-more-hours.html

177. Plain language is designed to ensure the reader understands a piece of writing as quickly, easily, and completely as possible. It avoids verbose, convoluted language and jargon. https://en.wikipedia.org/wiki/Plain_language; see also www.plainlanguage.gov, the US effort to clarify language in government agencies.

178. With thanks to Scrabble®.

179. Stephanie Sawchuk, "Steep Drops Seen in Teacher-Prep Enrollment Numbers," *Education Week*, October 21, 2014. See also Motoko Rich, "Across country, a scramble is on to find teachers," *New York Times,* August 10, 2015.

180. See note 40. Hale, "It's Not Easy Teaching Special Ed," NPR.

181. Jonathan Martin, "Blame Schools, Not Students, for the 'Failure of School Reform,'" *Connected Principals,* September 19, 2010, http://connectedprincipals.com/archives/880

182. Robert Samuelson, "School 'Reform' and Student Motivation," *Newsweek,* September 6, 2010, http://www.newsweek.com/school-reform-and-student-motivation-72173; and Amanda Ripley, "Motivation Matters More than Ever,"

*The Atlantic,* July/August 2013, http://www.theatlantic.com/magazine/archive/2013/07/motivation-matters-more-than-ever/309402/

183. Michael F. Giangreco, Susan W. Edelman, Tracy Evans Luiselli, Stephanie Z.C. McFarland, "Helping or Hovering? Effects of Instructional Assistant Proximity on Students with Disabilities," *Exceptional Children,* 64:1 (1997), pp. 7-18, http://maureenmcquiggan.com/files/Helping_or_Hovering.pdf

184. See note 108. Ginsburg, "Unlearning Learned Helplessness;" "What is Learned Helplessness?" *Edutopia,* August 29, 2011, http://www.edutopia.org/groups/special-ed/72044.

185. Dale Russakoff, "Schooled," *The New Yorker,* May 19, 2014.

186. Paul Tough, *Stanford Social Innovation Review,* May 31, 2016, http://ssir.org/articles/entry/helping_children_succeed_what_works_and_why

187. David Shenk, "The 32-Million Word Gap," *The Atlantic,* March 9, 2010, http://www.theatlantic.com/technology/archive/2010/03/the-32-million-word-gap/36856/; Margaret Talbot, "The Talking Cure," *The New Yorker,* January 12, 2015, and First 5 California, http://www.first5california.com/parents

188. Too Small to Fail, http://toosmall.org; "Doctors Enlisted in Early-Literacy Campaign," *Education Week,* January 21, 2015.

189. Joseph W. Gauld, "Parenting: The Key to America's Future," *Education Week,* December 1, 2010, p. 25; and Amanda Ripley, "Ban School Bake Sales," *Slate.com,* September 5, 2013, http://www.slate.com/articles/life/family/2013/09/ptas_and_bake_sales_why_volunteering_at_your_kid_s_school_does_not_make.html

190. See note 149. Ripley, *The Smartest Kids,* and, "Ban School Bake Sales," *Slate.com.* But see discussion of the ubiquitousness of PTAs in Japan, dating back to the US occupation 70 years earlier, in Eleanor Warnock and Yuka Koshino, "Japan's New Battlefront for Equality: The PTA," *Wall Street Journal,* July 30-31, 2016.

191. See note 177 discussion of plain language.

192. As a reminder, this discussion is about the 80-90% of students with mild/ moderate needs. We await results from the proposed task force for the 10-20% of students with profound/severe needs.

193. "Alexander: New Education Law Restores Control of Tennessee Classrooms to Tennesseans," http://www.alexander.senate.gov/public/index.cfm/ pressreleases?ID=A89B8A68-D2F2-410C-9BF3-022883738232

194. See note 193.

195. At the time of this writing, the Trump education effort appears to focus much discussion on parental choice through vouchers and charter schools. While these issues and controversies go far beyond this little book, it may be helpful to point out one distinction between special education's parental rights and the parental choice policies being considered, which, of course, include choice for parents of students with disabilities. In general, parental choice options provide parents with funds to help them choose other programs or schools for their children—both public and private. The options do not give parents the right to reject school programs or demand that schools create different programs for their children, as per the IDEA. In fact, current choice options for parents of students with disabilities generally include the requirement that parents waive their rights under the IDEA. See, e.g., Christina A. Samuels, "Vouchers Put Some Parents in Squeeze on Special Ed. Rights," *Education Week*, July 20, 2016. A complex topic for another day.

196. In 2003, the Government Accountability Office (GAO) estimated that there were five hearings per 10,000 students, equating to half of 1 percent. "Numbers of Formal Disputes Are Generally Low and States Are Using Mediation and Other Strategies to Resolve Conflicts," GAO Report to the Ranking Minority Member, Committee on Health, Education, Labor and Pensions, US Senate, September 2003, http://www.gao.gov/new.

items/d03897.pdf. The environment may become less attractive to due process, and it will reach a natural demise; that I call the "dinosaur effect." In its August 2014 report, the GAO cited the fact that the number of due process hearings between 2004 and 2014 decreased substantially due to declines in several states and the use of other dispute resolution options. "SPECIAL EDUCATION: Improved Performance Measures Could Enhance Oversight of Dispute Resolution," September 24, 2014, http://www.gao.gov/products/GAO-14-390

197. See note above. And see Nanette Asimov, "Extra-special education at public expense," *San Francisco Chronicle,* February 19, 2006.

198. Attorney Ronald Wenkart at Orange County Alliance event, May 20, 2016.

199. The reality of a system that has many settlements between schools and parents may work for parents who can contribute financially to their children's private school education or services. In such financial settlement agreements, schools and parents agree to pay part of the private bill. Thus, this common practice actually acts as a voucher system for parents who can "pay to play." See notes 46, 196, and 197.

200. "One System: Reforming Education to Serve All Students," *Report on California's Statewide Task Force on Special Education, March 2015,* http://www.smcoe.org/assets/files/about-smcoe/superintendents-office/statewide-special-education-task-force/Special_Ed_Task_Force_Report-reduced.pdf; "Special Education: A Service, not a Place," New Jersey School Boards Association (2014), https://www.njsba.org/news-information/research/njsba-task-force-on-special-education-report-2014/; and Christine A. Samuels, "Overhaul Urged to Aid Special Education in California," *Education Week,* March 24, 2015.

201. See note 8. Pudelski, *Rethinking…Due Process*, American Association of School Administrators.

202. http://www.israelnationalnews.com/News/Flash.aspx/264826

203. Special Education Day (December 2) is at http://specialeducationday. com/; see also, Sharon Otterman, "A Struggle to Educate the Disabled," *New York Times,* June 20, 2010, http://www.nytimes.com/2010/06/20/ education/20donovan.html?pagewanted=all&_r=0

204. "Inclusive Education," *UNESCO,* http://www.unesco.org/new/en/education/ themes/strengthening-education-systems/inclusive-education/single-view/ news/unesc

# Index

litigation, litigate, 26, 30, 40, 44, 59, 61, 65, 101, 109, 115, 117, 124

Living Room Conversations, 137

Lyon, G. Reid, 21

mainstreaming, mainstream, xvii, 35, 37, 44, 46-47, 97, 127, 131

Massachusetts, 40, 52, 60, 122

Mead, Margaret, 123

Meredith, Bruce and Julie Underwood, 51

Merriam-Webster, 55

mild, moderate needs, xix, 19, 22, 87, 93-94, 127, 133

modifications, xviii, 50, 55, 82-83, 98, 129, 132

Musgrove, Melody, 60

National Association of State Directors of Special Education, 61

National Assessment of Educational Progress (NAEP), 53

National Association for Gifted Children, 38

National Association of Secondary School Principals, 30, 61

National Center for Educational Statistics, 132

National Center for Learning Disabilities, 20

National Center on Educational Outcomes, 19

National Public Radio (NPR), 53, 59, 60, 109

New Jersey, 27, 117, 141

*New York Times*, 5, 53, 86, 126, 137

*Newsweek*, 110

No Child Left Behind Act (NCLB), 56, 61, 130, 132

NO Labels, 137

Obama, Barack, 39, 61, 76, 78, 121

objective, data, evidence, research, xvii, 16, 43, 45, 47, 49, 51, 90-91, 100, 127

Office of Special Education and Rehabilitative Services (OSERS), 38, 48, 132

Office of Special Education Programs (OSEP), 60, 132

Ounce of Prevention, 135

Palmaffy, Tyce, 28

parents, xi, xvii-xviii, xx-xxi, 3-5, 8, 13-14, 18, 20-32, 43-44, 48-49, 52, 54-55, 59, 64-66, 71, 74,

Made in the USA
San Bernardino, CA
19 June 2017